SEARCH for SODOM and GOMORRAH

By

Ralph E. Baney

1st Edition
3rd Printing

CAM PRESS
Kansas City, Missouri
1963

Library of Congress Catalog Card Number 61-18476

Copyright—1962 by Ralph E. Baney

Published by CAM Press
2000 Linwood Blvd.
Kansas City 9, Mo.

To Ruth and our sons
Ralph Jr., David and Phillip

*His Majesty King Hussein
of Jordan*

REVERIE

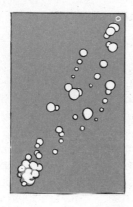

EVEN UNTO SODOM
AND GOMORRAH

The poisonous water drips from my face mask and seeps quickly into the dry sandy soil.

"The Dead Sea . . . Sodom and Gomorrah . . . What an adventure! Dr. Baney, now we know we're the only ones who've ever been in the Twin Sin Cities since they were destroyed." Dean turned and pointed as he spoke.

I sight along his arm. "See those blue-white clouds just over our marker buoy? They're our good-luck charms. And they'll be right there when we come back on the next expedition. Let's get these heavy tanks off and stow our gear."

I am only half-listening. The shore where we stand is at the base of a peninsula on the east bank. It looks just like a huge tongue. The clouds of evaporated salt water hug the surface of the sea as if reluctant to part company. The rocky, golden plains girdling the Dead Sea are dimming in the early evening dusk after the pale glare of the day. Our boat rides peacefully at anchor just below. The shadows creep over rippling waves, the white foam turns blue. The figures of my crew grow vague like those in a dream world.

For the moment I am in a reverie. A hundred times or more I have stood on this very shore, lost in the past and dreaming of the future. Countless times the same fantasy has fanned my wonder at the world buried beneath this sea into a white-hot desire to see it in reality. Looking out across this chemical cesspool, and with the hot sirocco wind stinging my face, I have seemed to hear two voices from far off. Sometimes the words have rung out, other times, just a whisper. But, always the same refrain: "We are down here, somewhere. Come, find us." Then the vision of the two lost cities slowly rising majestically in all their former ingloriousness.

And now at last, I believe I have found them. Not with my eyes, with my hands, because this Dead Sea has concealed them from man's vision. I have felt the roadway leading away from them, touched the wall which I believe is a part of them, and sifted through the mud of centuries that covers them to bring up artifacts and objects from these lost cities of perdition.

I have won; the goal has been reached; my venture has succeeded. As I stand here in the gathering gloom caught in the spell of the scene, the memories begin to ebb and flow much as the waves of the treacherous waters below.

What had brought me here? How had I dared to go to the bed of this sea of death? Why had the dream driven me on?

One does not undertake this kind of expedition without a restless desire and without being an expert master diver. My mind went back, back down through the years and the thousands of experiences to one particular day that seemed to be the start on the winding trail to this rocky shore and this thrilling moment.

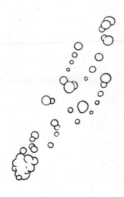

I. CAVALCADE

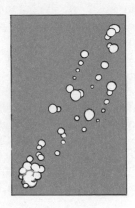

FROM THE BIG PINEY TO THE
"CRADLE OF CIVILIZATION"

I opened my eyes. The bright blazing sun
scornfully basted them into closing quickly. My
head ached with a muffled pounding; my heart
skipped and surged painfully. The mid-afternoon
cool breeze massaged my face while flashes of
thought skittered around inside my head. I gasped,
choked, sputtered.

I was coming back . . . suddenly I remembered! And gagged again! Terror clamped my throat shut like a noose slowly tightening. Yes, I remembered . . . The panic, the twisting and turning, the struggle to get to that pinpoint of air and light above me; then my lungs making their final gasp for air were filling with water, and the last impression before everything went dark and empty: the odd-shaped rocks covered with green slime outlined like shadowy castles . . . and the thought: Please, God, help me!

"Here now, boy! You all right, hey?" I turned my head slowly to squint upward. The man standing there looked down with a mixture of relief and annoyance on his craggy face. The leathery skin was wrinkled and heat-reddened. He looked familiar. Of course. The sheriff. But how, why, where . . .?

There was something clutched in my left hand. I started to turn over, but he put a warning touch to my arm. "Whoa, now, take it easy a minute. You gave me a scare, buddy. Good thing your pa had an idea you might be coming over to the Big Piney to explore some of these underwater caves today, or I might not have got to you in time." Then, with exasperation: "If you have to hold onto this fool notion about finding things under water, why do you have to go diving by yourself? Ain't you got no sense, boy?"

He meant well, I knew that. But, I guess I'd really given him quite a shock. And me, too! I was still trembling from that near brush with death.

I couldn't say anything. I was still half numb, yet ached all over. With his help I started to get up and snagged my swimming trunks on a sharp rock. The ripping sound, the hoarse breathing and anxious voice of the sheriff, the hot sun, the slapping of the river against the bank . . . these shook me awake. Scrambling to my feet, I stood shakily facing my rescuer.

The sheriff droned on. "Never thought your finding that cash register and check-writer in that old pond last week would start you off onto looking for other stuff. I'm proud that those things you found helped me corner that bank robber, but that don't mean you have to search every pond and river in this neck of the woods for me to catch other criminals. Better lay off, son. After what just happened, I'd say you're mighty lucky I came looking to tell you about the reward. I'd sure have hated to give your pa the bad news that his ten-year-old got too interested in diving and forgot to come up. If you're gonna go down that far, you better grow some gills."

My left hand still held something. I looked down at it. That old billfold! While the sheriff talked, the memory came back. That slippery piece of leather . . . there just a little deeper, just a little deeper . . . I can almost touch it . . . there, there, now! I've got it! . . . Hard to hold my breath . . . lungs aching . . . got to go up . . . got to . . . got to . . . oh, God, please help me . . .!

That's all I could remember. I was so ashamed at having pulled such a stunt that all I could do was to mumble my thanks to the kindly old man and stumble weakly homeward. His words echoed in my brain: ". . . grow gills like a fish, grow gills like a fish . . ."

When I got home and told my father what had happened, he first made sure I was all right, then gave me a lecture on the dangers in diving, especially alone. For awhile, after that, I steered clear of those tempting, cool green ponds, creeks and rivers around our home in southern Missouri. But, not for too long. That underwater world wouldn't let me rest. It was like an itch in the small of the back that couldn't be scratched. Every time I was alone, the visions of that new world held me in a trance. The fascination became too powerful; soon, I was at it again. Swimming, diving, exploring. But with more caution and fired with the idea of using something to help me stay down longer. Maybe something to help the breathing. Maybe something like the gills of a fish . . .?

The Big Piney River country in the Ozarks of southern Missouri is a wonderful place for swimming. All of us tow-heads worked hard in the fields most of the day and then dashed for the cold and clear streams all around. On a hot summer afternoon there was no better place to go. To the others, swimming was fun for its own sake; for me, it became an adventure-filled treasure hunt. While the others were racing or diving, I would float face down holding my breath and trying to see what was on the bottom. Usually there would be nothing more exciting than a crawdad scrambling backwards, a tadpole losing its tail, or a few fish swimming lazily. But my imagination pictured the scene with sunken pirate ships and lost cities beneath the seas.

I began to spend most of my free time in the water. My curiosity drove me on. Then, when I found the bank cash register and check-writer, my imagination burst its bounds, and I became bolder. I was sure that treasure of every kind lay waiting for me under water, any open water. If treasures could be found in this muddy, little pond, imagine what I could find at the bottom of rivers, seas, and oceans such as I was reading about in school! I couldn't rest; I had to find out, see these things, touch them.

These dreams, like a sharp hunger inside, drove me to trying to explore the caves in the Big Piney River. Diving off the high bluffs into the rushing clear waters was thrilling in itself, but peering into the cavernous openings underwater excited me more. The day of the accident found me there throwing caution to the winds and darting farther and farther down and in, like a puppy sniffing out the scent of rabbits. In my absorption, I hadn't noticed the branches of an old tree lurking in the gloom. It was when I tried to surface that I found my swimming trunks caught on a limb, and I almost paid a terrible price for my carelessness.

That experience shook me up, but when you're young and testing your strength and mind, it's hard to admit defeat. Besides, I couldn't get over wanting to find out what lay on the bottoms of the ponds and rivers.

The old sheriff's words began to sink home . . . "grow gills like a fish". I started to experiment with ways to stay down longer and in deeper water. I was determined to lick this problem.

My first underwater breathing invention was a length of garden hose. Lying on my back under water, with one end in my mouth and the other extending above the surface, I tried to suck in air. When this didn't work, I tried an inner tube. I sank it with stones, dived down next to it, and tried to inhale air from its valve. The tube won the fight. Next, I tried to share the air of a balloon. No better luck. Most of my early efforts were as useless as wings on a turtle, but I never stopped trying. And I wasn't the only one making these attempts; other divers, in other places and lands, led on by the same insatiable curiosity were going through the same maneuvers. That we all eventually succeeded is now a matter of record.

With all this experimentation and being in the water almost daily I might as well have been a fish. But, I was rapidly approaching manhood, and so, reluctantly I realized I would have to lay aside this childhood fascination and decide seriously what my future should be. My father, a minister, furnished the inspiration for my choice. I, too, would enter the ministry.

Following college and seminary, I was ordained in 1934. Then I received a scholarship to continue my studies in Palestine where I had the opportunity of pursuing my interest in archaeology at the American School of Oriental Research in Jerusalem. During this period I made many field trips.

That first year in Palestine and my new experiences made me fully aware of why this land is called the "cradle of civilization". Nearly every lonely mound or "tell" is steeped in cultural history. Layer upon layer awaits unpeeling by the methodical, patient archaeologist — the reconstructor of ancient man's life and times.

I could have thrown myself wholeheartedly into the study of archaeology, but there was a more pressing matter facing me. The Middle East, at that time, was a tinder-box awaiting a spark. There was unrest; population shift and economic dislocation were creating a poisonous climate in which hunger, suffering, and hardship became the daily lot of the poor. I could not turn a deaf ear and blind eye to the misery of my fellow man.

I halted my studies of archaeology and devoted myself to serving the needs of these people. My desire to minister was fulfilled, with God's help, by the establishment of the Holy Land Christian Approach Mission in Palestine. Since its founding in 1936, aid and comfort have been given to thousands, especially the orphans and crippled children in this land where Jesus walked.

My work in Palestine these past years has been soul-satisfying. However, God has provided other benefits. My dormant interest in archaeology has been awakened by contact, at every turn, with the evidences of Biblical history. This land is rich with reminders of long-dead civilizations, some of which have been unearthed by archaeologists. I have been especially drawn to the excavations of sites and towns located just as the Bible describes them. All of these places pulled at me, but I found myself attracted more and more to one particular area: The Dead Sea. Just looking at it, I became suspended; time and motion ceased, and my mind's eye saw it as it might have appeared in Bible days. What a glorious cavalcade of cities and characters paraded across the stage of the Dead Sea of long ago. What a scientific accomplishment it would be if I could discover artifacts, coins, fragments of bone and pottery and other evidences of these cultures of antiquity!

But aside from its archaeological interest, the Dead Sea's place in the emergence of Christendom gave it a strong emotional appeal as a site for exploration. Nineteen hundred years before the birth of Christ, as recorded in Genesis 13:10, Abraham, Isaac, Jacob and Lot pitched their tents at its southern end. In ancient times the Sea did not extend so far south as it does today. South of the "tongue", the peninsula which juts out into the sea west of Kir-Haresth on the eastern side, was the Vale of Siddim. (Gen. 14:3). Most archaeologists believe that the five cities of the plain—Sodom, Gomorrah, Admah, Zeboiim, Zora—were located here.

Moses, leading the children of Israel out of Egypt to the Promised Land after 40 years of wandering in the wilderness, chose a route skirting the south and eastern shores of the Dead Sea and across the Mountains of Moab. Permitted only to gaze upon the land of Canaan from afar, Moses viewed the Dead Sea from the lofty heights of Mt. Nebo, later, his tomb. Joshua and his army stormed the walls of Jericho, just north of the Dead Sea, 1200 to 1300 years before the birth of Christ, to open the way for the conquest of Canaan. Herod the Great constructed a theater, palace, and citadels at Jericho during his reign and sailed the waters of the Dead Sea to reach the hot springs on the eastern shore where he bathed as a cure for his illness, believed to be cancer. It was here near the Dead Sea in the Jordan River that Christ was baptized by John the Baptist, and here overlooking the Dead Sea on a mountain the Son of God faced temptation. Also, in this region, Jesus spent the last few weeks of his public ministry before traveling to Jerusalem for the observances of Passover. John the Baptist was taken prisoner and sent by Herod Antipas to a mountain-top fortress overlooking the Dead Sea to be executed.

Every time I visited the Dead Sea region, I realized that man's knowledge of these people and the glorious events of their lives was incomplete; I became obsessed with the desire to bring the past and present into closer focus.

The finding of the Dead Sea Scrolls further crystallized this desire. The Scrolls were discovered in that area known as Khirbet Qumran on the northwestern shore of the Dead Sea by a Bedouin boy looking for a goat. Ruins of a Jewish monastic order known as the Essenes had been uncovered here and systematically explored. It is believed that the Scrolls were copied by scribes in the Qumran monastery from books of the Old Testament. Sealed in clay jars, they were hidden in the surrounding caves, protected against the elements and safe from enemies. The Scrolls have given us definite proof of the truth of the Scriptures.

This new-found knowledge of the Bible in which the Dead Sea had played so vital a role turned me from dreaming to action. Action which eventually brought me back to this area, filled my life with adventure, and gave me the chance to fulfill my dream.

I decided to form an expedition. With the latest equipment and procedures, together with all the skill I had developed in my earlier efforts in underwater exploration, I would dive beneath these waters and locate Sodom and Gomorrah.

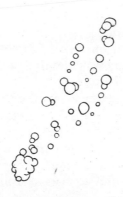

II. CHALLENGE

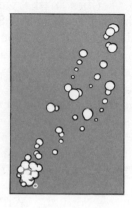

DOWN A LONG ROAD OF OBSTACLES

Organizing an expedition so that it will be successful is not an undertaking to be approached impulsively. Preparations must be thorough and complete. Attending to every detail proves to be a rigorous, demanding ordeal.

At the outset, there were unique problems presented by the Dead Sea in penetrating its twenty-seven per cent salt water barrier and in probing its depths. Research, study, experimentation, and testing of equipment and methods under approximately similar conditions had to be carefully conducted.

Take the equipment for a starter. The expedition would require specialized types, some just beyond the experimental stage. Other men besides myself had, in modern times, been drawn to the mysterious depths and had been trying to solve the problems of pressure, temperature, and density of the great oceans and seas. Each attempt had resulted in modifications of earlier equipment until, today, man has almost conquered this element so foreign to his natural habitat.

The story of man's effort to perfect underwater diving equipment is a long and thrilling one, filled with courage and derring-do. Suffice it here to say that the fascination for underwater exploration probably started in ancient times. One has but to recall the 38th chapter of Job in which the Lord, appearing out of a whirlwind, challenges Job with these questions:

"Who shut up the sea with doors? . . . saying hitherto shalt thou come but no further; and there shall thy proud waves be stayed? . . . Hath the rain a father? . . . and out of whose womb came the ice? . . . Canst thou lift up thy voice to the clouds, that abundance of waters may cover thee?. . . Who can number the clouds in wisdom or who can stay the bottles of Heaven?"

Not only did Job find the questions imponderable in his day but, also, men throughout all ages have sought the answers. After all, water covers almost seventy-five per cent of our globe and presents both mystery and challenge.

Ancient history left many records of man curiously searching for greater knowledge of the seas and its denizens. Aristotle was the first pioneer marine biologist. Natural diving in the lakes, seas, and oceans had been practiced for sport, to augment food supplies, and to aid in waging war since time began. But as societies progressed and changed from primitive agrarian types to a more sophisticated urban nature, the early crude makeshift apparatus no longer suited man's purposes. As far back as 900 B.C., architects made bas-reliefs and engravings to indicate that even in those times man was already attempting to develop equipment which would make it possible for him to remain under water for longer periods of time than only his own lungs would allow. Early day artists drew weird designs for such equipment and left them in old manuscripts.

Bridging the years and countless efforts to invent practical means and methods for men to dive and maneuver freely and safely under water, in 1943 a French scientist, Captain Jacques Consteau, perfected the first self-contained underwater breathing apparatus which he dubbed SCUBA. This contrivance used cylindrical tanks of compressed air, with an attached regulator to automatically adjust the air pressure to the diver's requirements. The diver breathed through a rubber mouthpiece held tightly between his teeth, and the regulator automatically increased the air pressure to equalize pressures inside the body with mounting water pressure from the outside.

Other related equipment, such as the diving mask and flexible rubber foot-flippers, were patterned after similar equipment used for centuries. These, too, were modernized and perfected by another Frenchman and used with the Consteau-Gagnan Aqua-Lung, enabling the diver to turn, twist, and swim in any direction.

With the invention and perfection of SCUBA, here was the equipment the world had been waiting for. The ways and means were now at hand for the study and exploration of hidden secrets of the underwater world. Many, for the first time, swam along with the fish and dived down into the shadowy depths through filtered light into a weightless, silent, and mysteriously beautiful world.

Many men in all walks of life began to use this equipment. Among them were swimmers—sportive or treasure-hunting—and geologists, archaeologists, and oceanographers following their scientific bent toward accumulation of knowledge.

The oceanographer found in free diving a new medium in which he studied and charted the flow of the seas and followed the underwater currents. He discovered many phenomena, including a river of sand constantly flowing on the bed of the ocean just as a large stream of water flows above the ground.

In tropical waters, biologists soared around beds of jewelled, multicolored coral, studying marine life: fishes as colorful as exotic flowers, and the millions of other sea creatures.

My first experience in gaining a practical knowledge of SCUBA diving was in the largest of our midwestern lakes, known as the Lake of the Ozarks. This is a lovely man-made lake one hundred and fifty miles southeast of Kansas City, Missouri. I shall never forget my first dive from a rocky shore into water more than fifty feet deep. As I descended gradually into this new world beneath the surface, I was thrilled to find that I could suspend myself in "space", or with a movement of my flipper, I could move in any direction at will. I was again experiencing my first tantalizing glimpse of the underwater wonderland. Rocks covered with soft brown algae looked ghostly in the shimmering filtered sunlight, and I found that fish, especially the smaller ones swimming together, were seemingly unafraid.

My diving "buddy" on a great number of dives was an ex-Marine named Dean Ryther, also from Kansas City. He and I have searched the depths of this lake and explored caves and flooded forests which were once the haunts of deer and foxes but where now only fish abound. Together we have hunted and speared fish and shared other exploratory experiences under water.

Dean, as a diving partner, has been invaluable. He is president of the Kansas City Frogmen's Club and a diving instructor. We have collaborated on several underwater salvage operations over the last three years. Among various articles we have recovered are wallets, dentures, glasses, motors, a cabin cruiser, and the ejected seat of a B-47 Jet bomber which had buried itself in mud sixty feet under the surface of the water. On one occasion we plunged through ice in freezing temperatures for five successive days before finally raising a ten-ton cabin cruiser.

But all divers need the services of others if they are to survive. And Dean's wife, Dorothy Ann, is another of the ever-increasing army of "water-widows" who patiently wait on the surface, watching the bubbles, ready and waiting with towels and hot coffee for her diver's return from the world down under. Dot is an experienced "tenderman" (or "tenderwoman" as she prefers to be called) — a caretaker of the diving equipment, a sort of diver's valet. Five feet two, Dot can harness a diver with his tank, clean his face mask, and hand him his flippers faster than most "tendermen" I know. She, too, has proved to be most valuable.

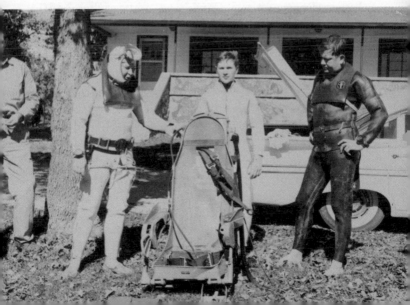

Having laid the groundwork for the expedition by practicing with the SCUBA equipment and gaining needed experience in its use underwater, we began our study and research in earnest, both while working in connection with the Mission in Jordan, and in the United States. In Jordan, I visited the American School of Oriental Research and the Rockefeller Museum, talking with officials and studying the finds of archaeologists, in particular, the topography of the Khirbet Qumran area adjacent to the shores of the Dead Sea where the famous scrolls had been found.

In addition, I studied the technical aspects, methods, equipment and diversified problems of underwater expeditions previously carried out by explorers, oceanographers, and treasure-hunters in Mediterranean waters off the coasts of France, Greece, Spain, in the Caribbean and in the Pacific Ocean off the California coast. Records were becoming more plentiful; with SCUBA so perfected that man could safely descend into the depths, underwater expeditions were being directed more and more to the interests of science. And I felt certain that exploring the waters of the Dead Sea would add still more valuable historical and scientific data.

As I continued my preparations, research, and study, I learned that having the proper knowledge and equipment was not all I needed for the expedition. I had, also, to secure permission from the proper authorities. Consequently, I requested authorization from the Jordanian government to carry out our expedition in the Dead Sea. This turned out to be not so simple. SCUBA diving or any similar underwater gymnastics was something quite unknown in this country. My proposal, outlined in letters to various individuals there, was received with skepticism.

For example, one of the persons to whom I broached the subject was the business manager of the Christian Approach Mission, Mike Handal, of Bethlehem. He prides himself on being quite "western-minded". Mike spent his early youth in San Antonio, Texas, and likes to think that he is in tune with everything new in the United States. During the baseball season he avidly follows the fortunes of the New York Yankees on his shortwave radio. And his most fervent desire is to one day bring his family to America. Yet, when I told him of my proposed expedition to the Dead Sea, his reaction was mainly amazement. The responses I got from others in Jordan to whom I had outlined my program were similar to Mike's.

He wrote to me: "I know that you always want to go many times to the Dead Sea when you are in Jordan. I have told you many times that I will go with you whenever you want to go here. But now you tell me you are going to dive in the Dead Sea! Never! How are you going to get under the water in the first place? You know, we sit on this water and read the Jerusalem Times. And to get the Dead Sea water in your eyes or to choke on it is to suffer agony. You will pardon my writing such words to my Director, Sir, but as we say in Arabic—I believe you know the word—I think you must be "mishnoon" (*crazy*)! Dr. Baney, if you were to tell me that you are going to ride a camel across the Dead Sea, I could believe it more than I could believe you were going down to the very bottom of the Sea!"

He also wrote that he had discussed my proposed Dead Sea Expedition with Ayoub Mussalam, the Mayor of Bethlehem, and with numerous other officials and friends in Jordan. All were incredulous and unbelieving. The concensus was that Dr. Baney must be "mishnoon" to think he could dive in the Dead Sea.

It took a great deal of correspondence with government officials and those in favor with the "powers that be" to secure the necessary permits in the face of this skepticism. However, the official notification came through, signed by the Minister of Education and Antiquities, His Excellency, Mohammed Amin Shanquity. It was dated October 1, 1959, and read as follows:

"I hereby authorize Dr. Ralph Baney, Director General of the Christian Approach Mission of Kansas City, U.S.A., to undertake a diving expedition to the bottom of the Dead Sea in the Lisan area in search of the probable site of Sodom and Gomorrah. This authorization is valid until the thirty-first day of March, 1960."

Then I set out to convince Dean and Dot Ryther that I needed them on this expedition. Dean listened carefully as I outlined my proposal, took a deep breath, and said in typically measured words, "Dr. Baney, I'll dive with you in the Ozarks, or in any sea in the world, but I just don't like that name—Dead Sea!" I offered to call it the "Sea of Salt" but this brought only another question from him. "Why should we dive in this Dead Sea when there are sunken ships and all kinds of treasures in other seas much easier to dive in?" I repeated that we were going to look for special sunken cities which are relatively rare in seas throughout the world. As I talked, I could sense that Dean was remembering his early Sunday School lessons, particularly those about Sodom and Gomorrah. Finally, after I had pointed out the joys of seeing new places plus the glamour and excitement of traveling in the Middle East, Dean and Dot glanced at each other as if to seek mutual confirmation, and I knew I had convinced them of the merit of the expedition. Dot went in search of an Atlas to pinpoint the location of the Dead Sea. While the girls discussed what kind of clothing would be suitable for this kind of expedition, Dean and I retired to the basement to look over our equipment.

Later we talked far into the night, dreaming and planning. The question arose as to whether Ruth should come along. Although she has dived with me in the Lake of the Ozarks and other waters and enjoys underwater exploration, we felt that it would be out of the question to obtain leaves of absence from the Mission in Kansas City for both Ruth and myself. Besides, I felt that the work of the expedition would be, perhaps, too rigorous and trying for her.

As for me, our Board graciously granted a three months leave of absence to initiate the Dead

Sea Expedition with the provision that I spend part of my time working at the Mission in Bethlehem.

It was not quite so easy for Dean and Dot to get away. Both worked for Southwestern Bell Telephone Company, which did not consider this expedition related to their business. However, after much persuasion, they were given the desired leaves. For a while it was like pulling petals from a daisy: They can go—they can't—they can go—they can't—they can!

Next came the decision of when to start the expedition. This was not too difficult. In the first place, during the summer months — from May through September—the temperatures rise to unbearable heights in this lowest spot on the globe. Everyone visiting the area during this season must be prepared to endure the extreme heat.

Secondly, from October to January the activities at Mission headquarters make it imperative that I be there. It is difficult for me to get away at this time of year, so, taking these two facts into account, I decided to launch the Dead Sea Expedition around the first of February. This would be the rainy season in Jordan, but we reasoned that a few drops of water couldn't seriously hamper an underwater exploration.

From the time of deciding when the Expedition would start, we spent many a night into the morning hours listing our equipment and other necessities for a successful project. It began to be apparent that we had seriously underestimated the cost of the expedition. We had to cull the list and keep only to absolute essentials. This is the list decided upon after much deliberation:

1. One electric and one gas compressor with oil for engine.
2. One Bendix Sonar depth fathom recorder.
3. One transducer with power supply, cord and two indicators for depth recorder.
4. One Sea-Tow Shark for underwater propulsion.
5. One Sea-Tow Minnow — smaller version of Shark.
6. One Dictaphone, transformer and belts for recording purposes.
7. Six sets neoprene rubber, both wet and dry suits.
8. Several face masks, sets of fins, underwater compasses, depth gauges, watches, knives, gloves, hoods, life-jackets, weight belts, extra parts and repair kits, etc.
9. Two double Aqua-Lung tanks, blocks, and two single tanks.
10. One large filter.
11. Six regulators, pressure gauges and tools for repairing.
12. One pair binoculars.
13. 35-mm. camera and 16-mm. movie camera with film and flash bulbs.
14. Tools for underwater work.
15. Plenty of old clothing.

Of course we had plenty of old clothing and some of the equipment, but much of it had to be new and was not easy to obtain. We dared not

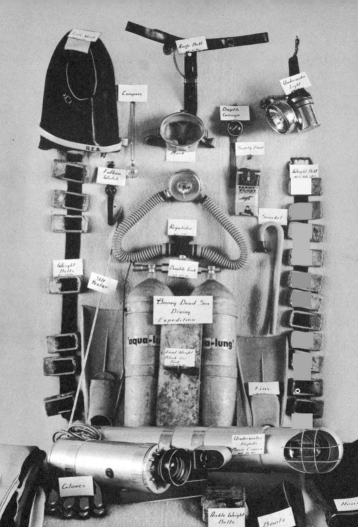

Life Vest

Knife Belt

Underwater Light

Compass

Depth Gauge

Mask

Safety Float

R.F.D.

Pulham Watch

Snorkel

Weight Belt

Regulator

Weight Belts

Self Tester

Double Tank

Baney Dead Sea
Diving
Expedition

'aqua-lung'   'a-lung'

Lead Weight
About 5 oz
Feet

Fins

Underwater
torpedo
Power Camera

Dive Suit

Gloves

Ankle Weight
Belts

Boots

Hood

Sea-Tow

risk our lives using old equipment in this treacherous Sea where no man up to now will have dived. Dean and I both agreed that we must have completely new and modern equipment. By contacting the various supply houses all over the United States and in Europe, we were able to obtain some of the needed equipment free to test for advertising purposes. We were able to convince the manufacturers that their products would be put to the most rigorous and hazardous use.

After all, no equipment has been tested in waters comparable to the Dead Sea. A number of manufacturers cooperated with us. Among them were: U.S. Divers Company, Bulow Electric Company, Marine Division of Bendix Aviation Company, and Wilfred O. White and Sons.

Now we had some of our equipment and the necessary permit; we had passed the initial stage in our planning. The expedition was taking shape.

III. CARAVAN TO ADVENTURE

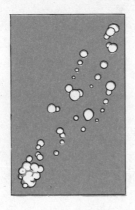

THE WAY AHEAD

With the preliminary planning out of the way, the full financing, shipping of equipment, arranging our itinerary and the actual trip now have to be managed. There are authorities I want to consult and other equipment to add. I go into high gear.

Now we tackle the job of inventorying and checking the equipment. Since it is arriving from various parts of the country and from Europe, we must be extra careful to make sure all component parts have been delivered and repacked for overseas shipment. Each piece is important. The success of the whole expedition might hinge on one small item at a crucial moment. Dot Ryther becomes indispensable in handling these details.

When the last items have been packed, the total weight comes to 1200 lbs. Through the generosity of the Scandinavian Airlines System, the equipment is airlifted from the United States to Jordan.

We are ready for the trip. And, although we hesitate to release any publicity about our plans, the local press does run a story on the expedition. Later, in New York, we are met by a battery of reporters. This happens again when we arrive in Paris and also in Cannes, France, where I want to consult one of the authorities I had in mind.

January 31, 1960, dawns clear and cold. The exciting moment is here. There are four in our party who take off from Kansas City into the New Year with its promise of high adventure. We leave amid the good wishes for our success from the "Mission" members and our own families being left behind. Dean and Dot Ryther are going as master diver and technical assistant, and Miss Viola Conway is traveling with us on an assignment for the Mission in our Orphan Home in Bethlehem.

We are to board our SAS plane for the Middle East in New York City, but first I stop over in Baltimore for a conference with Dr. William F. Albright, professor emeritus at Johns Hopkins University, a renowned archaeologist and Bible scholar.

Dr. Albright was on the staff of the American School of Oriental Research in Jerusalem from 1919 to 1936, serving as director for thirteen years. While there, he directed and assisted in many excavations and expeditions, including surveys around the periphery of the Dead Sea. Being an authority and expert on the Semitic languages, he also was the first scholar to translate sections of the Dead Sea Scrolls. He has written over 800 articles and books, many of which I have studied. I looked forward eagerly to our meeting.

He greeted me graciously. During our talk, Dr. Albright filled me in with a first-hand account of many of his experiences. In his approach to the historical events of the civilizations around the Dead Sea, he made it sound as though the happenings were as recent as the news in the morning papers. I had never before heard history made so alive.

We discussed my expedition, and he gave me some valuable advice on methods of charting and mapping the topography of the bed of the Dead Sea. Our coring operations got a going-over, too. Then he urged me, if I did nothing else, to map the bottom of the Dead Sea. I said I would and that I hoped we would also find objects of archaeological value. He offered a suggestion on the possible location of the cities of Sodom and Gomorrah. He said he favored the southeast corner.

After a further review of my plans, I said good-by to this warm, helpful man whose knowledge and experience have helped so much. His advice and encouragement remain one of the high spots of the expedition.

On leaving Dr. Albright, I rejoined my party. We leave Baltimore, stop in New York for the SAS plane, and head for Paris with high hopes and spirits rising.

The flight across is routinely uneventful, and soon we touch down in Paris. In every field of endeavor, there are authorities and experts to turn to for accurate and detailed information. Before starting on the trip, I had determined to consult with two of these men. One, Dr. Albright, I had just left; the other was Monsieur Rebikoff. In Paris we meet Monsieur Dimitri Rebikoff and his versatile wife Ada, a most charming and hospitable couple. Mrs. Rebikoff invites us to their lovely villa in Cannes. It is situated on a finger of land jutting out into the Mediterranean. Her husband's office seems to be in the sea which encloses the villa on three sides.

Dimitri Rebikoff is one of the foremost engineers in the invention of miniature submarine and electronic lighting equipment for underwater photography and exploration. One of his spectacular inventions—the Torpedo—makes underwater mobility faster and easier. Besides inventing, Monsieur Rebikoff builds vital apparatus for the navies of the NATO countries. I hoped to get the latest equipment from his factory, as I had been told by the U.S. Navy that his latest models would not be available in the U.S. for some time. All in all, I felt that this man could be of great help in outfitting our expedition with the type of equipment needed for maximum results.

After quickly refreshing ourselves at the villa, Dean and I spend several hours going through the Rebikoff plant, looking over his latest equipment and machinery. One day has been arranged for diving and trying out the Pegasus, a powerful new miniature submarine with two brilliant lights for underwater photography. The sea is too rough that day, so we have to be content with a demonstration on the pier.

Our three-day stay at Cannes is most rewarding. Monsieur Rebikoff gives us the benefit of his advice and suggestions for our expedition; but most important, he lets us have two of the latest and most modern underwater cameras.

Leaving Cannes, we fly on to Rome, then Beirut, over to Lebanon and across the Lebanese range to Jordan. This is familiar territory to me. In the distance, I glimpse the Sea of Galilee and catch an

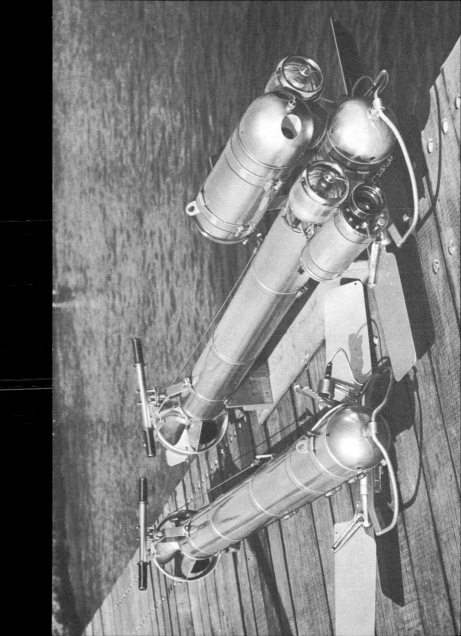

overall view of the country to its far horizons. Excitement mounts in each of us as we near our final destination at Amman, capitol city of Jordan. Dean and I go over the instruction manuals to the new equipment again.

"Dr. Baney, I don't see any roads or towns down there. Is this whole country desert?", Dot asks, with a note of anxiety in her voice.

"Be patient, Dot. This part of the country is rather barren, but Amman is a large city of over 200,000. Watch and you'll see green foliage around the Jordan valley. . . . There it is, out the window to the right."

Sure enough, there below is the Jordan valley with its thick growth of oleanders and rushes along

the banks of the river. We follow the tortuous wind-
ings of the river until it disappears in the distant
haze. "Ah," I announce, "the Dead Sea! The spot on
the map we've been looking at for so long."

We are all too excited to talk as we crowd close
to the double-paned windows looking out on the im-
mense panorama spread below. There is the Sea,
indeed, that mysterious plain of deep blue water,
capped this morning with white foam whipped up
by the wind. There, too, is the Jordan Delta, constantly moving in on the Sea as tons of mud and silt
are swept along by its swift current.

Dot and Dean are suddenly full of questions as
the plane rocks in the turbulent air over the Jordan
valley, and we take our seats to fasten the seat belts.

"I thought the Sea was supposed to have risen some twenty feet in the last hundred years or so", ventures Dean. "It looks as though it's receding instead."

"Yes, the Sea bed is supposed to be rising all the time, Dean. Thousands of tons of sand are blown into the Sea every year by the desert winds. But, they've had a severe drought here these past three years, so the water level is lower than it has been for a long time."

Dot asks if this desolate area north of the Dead Sea has ever been fertile. "Yes", I tell her, "in Biblical times this area was quite lush. Don't you remember, the children of Israel camped here for several years, possibly before going on into the land of Canaan. They didn't have a modern asphalt road to travel on like the one below us, nor an airport like the new one we will land at in Amman."

This is the first time I will arrive in the Holy Land in a dual capacity: Director of the Mission and an "oceanographer". The landing is almost due, and we feel overselves tightening. The rest of the party looks somewhat bewildered, and I have the sudden thought that any second one of them is going to blurt, "Let's turn around and go home!" But no one does, and our spirits quicken as we watch the landing strip awaiting the plane's approach. The hostess announces in both Arabic and English that we are landing at Amman and would we be kind enough to have our passports ready.

I am always thrilled on my return to the land where Jesus walked. In the years of our work here we have made many warm friends, and this land has really become a second home to Ruth and me. In the crowd waiting for the passengers, there are many familiar faces. Scrambling to get coats, hats, brief cases, maps, magazines, cameras, and all the many items one travels with, we do not have much chance to find out just who is waiting for us beyond the "Customs" sign. Mike has already smoothed the way for us, however, and we breeze through the formalities to be greeted with typical Arab salutations—hearty handshakes and kisses on both cheeks.

Among the people greeting us is our very good friend, the Honorary Director of the Christian Approach Mission in Jordan, Tewfic Pasha Kattan. The Pasha is distinguished in his country for his philanthropies and unselfish interest in helping the poor. He is from Bethlehem where our Mission is centered and is a member of Parliament from that district. He has been most helpful to the Mission, and in the early stages of the expedition his assistance was invaluable.

"It is good to have you back again, Dr. Baney", says the Pasha in greeting. "I welcome you and your friends to Amman. Come now and have an Arabic coffee."

Now, Dot does not even drink American coffee. Picture her first try at drinking the thick, bitter Arabic blend. Not wanting to offend, Dot takes the tiny cup of steaming brew and sniffs delicately. Almost immediately her big blue eyes seek mine with the look of a small puppy about to be put out-doors for the night. I shake my head, and she obediently takes a sip. Poor girl, I know it takes all her self-control to drink that ounce of Arabic coffee, but she downs most of it and therewith quali-fies for the good-conduct medal.

We take our leave from the Pasha to go to the hotel and arrange to meet him the next day for the first of several visits to the officials of Jordan. Now that we are finally at the scene of operations, the expedition is beginning to gather momentum. Soon, we hope, the actual diving will begin.

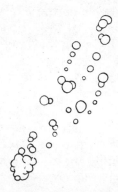

IV. PROTOCOL

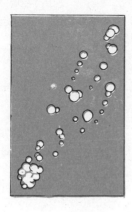

PROCEDURES PORTRAYED

In the early morning sunlight Amman sparkles like a crystal chandelier. The reflected beams of the sun bounce from window to window, rooftop to rooftop, until the whole city seems bathed in fire. Here, in the older part of the city, the crisp, cold air whisks around the narrow winding streets, carrying with it is the unmistakable odors of baked concrete, camel dung, motor car gasoline fumes, spicy cooking, and ripened fruit. The sonorous chant of the muezzin (holy man) pounds the eardrums as he calls the inhabitants to worship. The barking of dogs swells to a crescendo, roosters set up the cock-a-doodle-doo's, donkeys bray loudly, people pop out of doorways, auto horns toot; voices rise and fall in traditional bargaining; and life moves swiftly into another day.

Dean and I shivering in our thin clothes, push through the thoroughfare, already overcrowded with camels, motor-cars, vendors, carts and people. We are going to the office of the Pasha, my friend of long-standing, without whose help I would have been stymied. The Pasha, although not a government official, is held by them in the highest esteem. More than once, in my years of work in the Mission, I have called upon this good man to intercede on our behalf when a misunderstanding had arisen or some other difficulty has had to be resolved. Not once had he failed me—nor did he on this occasion, by offering his valuable assistance and suggestions.

In Jordan, protocol or proper procedures in dealing with people is highly important. Not following these procedures can cause embarrassment if not actually creating resentment. The officials might even take the attitude that a foreigner who would not take the trouble to familiarize himself with the local customs is showing contempt for them and thus is being discourteous. In our case, protocol did not present a problem. The good Pasha, acting as my intermediary, public relations man, often interpreter and guide, helped pave the way for us smoothly.

When we reach his handsomely furnished office, he greets us warmly. He is tremendously interested in our project and eager to help start the ball rolling. But, as protocol demands, first we spend at least ten minutes asking about each other's health and family. Then, the Pasha sends for a servant who brings in a tray of sweets. This action apparently signifies that the introductory phase of the meeting is over, and now the real business is ready to be taken up.

"Dr. Baney, may I make a suggestion?" he says, as Dean and I make ourselves comfortable in the well-padded chairs around his desk.

"Please do," I tell him.

"Very well, then. I think it would be wise if, first you go to call on Dr. Dejani, who is, as you know, the Director of the Department of Antiquities. Obviously, he will be quite interested in the details of your plan, as any finds will naturally be examined and catalogued by his department. Do not be offended by the many questions he will ask, he will thus be showing his great respect for you and this expedition which we all hope will be a tremendous success".

I assure the Pasha that I am willing to answer all questions freely and am anxious to secure the cooperation of Dr. Dejani. He reaches for the telephone and dials the office of the Director of the Department of Antiquities.

The arrangement is made, and then with an other signal, the Pasha summons a servant who brings in the tray of Turkish coffee. This hospitality marks the end of business. I have found the procedures in the Pasha's office are followed almost invariably the same way in other meetings with dignitaries.

After the coffee, we take the short trip to Dr. Dejani's office in the Pasha's limousine. Arriving there, Dean and I are formally introduced to the Director, exchange the preliminaries, have our sweets, and then proceed to a discussion of the expedition. As the Pasha had said they would, the questions came immediately. Dr. Dejani obviously wants to find out all he can about our project. His are the first of many questions put to us by other dignitaries we met later, and, I must say, I was highly impressed by how quickly they grasped the essentials of my plan. The more technical details presented some difficulty, but eventually, everyone at these higher levels in the government became fully informed about the expedition.

As we answer the Director's questions, occasionally the Pasha speaks up, in his eagerness to be of help to expand on some point I have made. All the conversation takes place in a very congenial atmosphere, and harmony is evident. Dr. Dejani appears satisfied with the information, although he is not too familiar with undersea diving procedures. He keeps coming back to wondering how we can possibly dive under such foul waters, do research, and stay for any length of time. I assure him we are fully qualified divers and will not risk our lives or the success of the expedition with any but the best equipment. Then he says, "Would you like to meet His Excellency, Mohammed Amin Shanquity, the Minister of Education? I know he will be pleased to hear personally of your plans."

"I am most anxious to see the Minister and thank him for the license for the expedition. Of course, he also will want complete details of the project." I tell the Director. "We would be very happy to have you accompany us, Dr. Dejani."

The Director expresses his thanks for the invitation, picks up the telephone, calls the office of the Minister, and makes the arrangement. The Pasha's limousine is waiting, we enter and arrive at the office of the Minister of Education in just a few minutes.

Here, a cordial reception is given us, and after the usual exchange of courtesies, His Excellency gets to the point of the meeting. He is as full of questions as an M. C. on a quiz program. In spite of the inquiries, the Minister directs the conversation in such a way that we are completely at ease. He is quite charming and very shrewd. He listens intently as I outline my proposal and then shows great interest in the coring operations part of our project.

I have explained to him that our general procedures fall in three main phases. First we explore the terrain of the sea by charting the bottom, using our Sonar Recording System. This gives us the topography of the area. If the Sonar pictures any mass which does not conform to the regular pattern of this section of the bottom, it is recorded on a graph in a series of long wavy lines, similar to the marking of impulses picked up by a lie-detector. Then comes phase two. At this stage of exploration, we dive to these unusual masses to try to discover what they contain and if any objects can be found in their vicinity. The final, or third stage, is the coring. Simply stated, this is the method for recovering coins, pieces of pottery, bones, tools, etc., embedded in these masses, by driving hollow six-inch wide pipes down and in about six feet until the ends are stuffed with the sediment. The pipes are then raised, and the stuffings, or "cores" are removed for inspection.

The minister, with a straight face and a twinkle in his eye, asks,

"Do you think you might bring up some black gold (oil) in one of these cores? Oh well, no matter the color, so long as it is gold."

I laugh and say, "What I hope to find may not be black gold or white gold, but it surely will lead to gold coming into the country."

He understands perfectly.

The Minister then assures me that I can depend on his complete cooperation and wants to be notified of any unusual finds. He receives my promise that anything of significance will be reported to him immediately.

The good-bye coffee is placed at our disposal, and the reception comes to an end. Dean and I are taken back to the hotel by the Pasha. There we bid him goodbye and go up to our rooms.

It has been a tiring but exciting day. We are making progress in meeting the right people, but there is still much to be done. So far, I have gotten offers of cooperation, but I need much concrete aid before we can start the actual diving.

Late this afternoon Dr. Dejani calls to remind me of our appointment and the interview he has arranged for us with the Director of the Department of Tourism, Asem Al Taji, at the Amman Broadcasting station. He apologizes for reminding me so late in the day, but we both realize how important this publicity can be to the expedition.

Naturally, any finds will attract tourists in even greater numbers to this kingdom. I thank him for calling, and prepare for our evening interview. Upon our arrival we learned that His Excellency the Prime Minister, Hazza Majali, was there for a broadcast, accompanied by his charming wife.

The Director takes us into an ante-room opposite the broadcasting booths and introduces me to His Excellency and his charming wife. He tells me he has heard a great deal of our expedition and wants to learn more about it first-hand.

"I'll give you as clear a picture as I can." I tell him.

During the conversation he informs me that his home is near Karak, south of Amman and one of the larger towns to the east of the Dead Sea. Naturally, he is familiar with the region and for that reason is quite enthusiastic about our trip there.

I pull out the working map Ruth had drawn for us in Kansas City. It just so happens I have it with me. It becomes quite a conversation piece with everyone who sees it, and the Prime Minister is no exception. He becomes absorbed in studying it.

"Your Excellency," I say, "I wonder if you would do me a favor and point out three areas in the Dead Sea you think might yield something of importance." He smiles his agreement and looks over the map closely.

I have a reason for asking this favor. In my conference with Dr. Albright in Baltimore, I had asked him to show me on this same map where he thought the lost cities might have been located. He had chosen the Lisan area where perennial tributaries flow into the Dead Sea as the most likely spot. Now, I am curious to see what opinion the Prime Minister has.

His Excellency takes his pen in hand saying, "The lost cities could have been here," makes a mark, "—or here", (second mark), "—or here", and with a flourish, autographs the margin HAJ MAJALI 13-2-60. He has marked the same areas Dr. Albright had pointed out! The map is now among my treasured mementoes of the expedition.

The meeting ends with his expressing the desire to be informed of our progress. After the broadcast with the Director of Tourism, we leave the Station and return to the hotel.

The breaks are certainly going our way. I could hardly have hoped for success in the expedition without the good wishes of these officials.

But the expedition was not so readily approved by everyone in Jordan. There was a certain amount of publicity in the local press concerning our arrival and some reporting on our progress in the expedition and our hopes of locating the lost cities. Some of the articles were objective and factual. Others reflected a minority attitude; this was a foolish adventure undertaken by a group of American thrill-seekers.

In support of the uninformed lunatic fringe ideas, the press played up a theory by a Comrade

Agrest, a physico-mathematician from Moscow. His explanation was that the sin-sodden cities of Sodom and Gomorrah were destroyed by a nuclear explosion triggered by creatures from outer space when they jettisoned their surplus nuclear fuel. He even went so far as to state that the spacemen had carved the 2000 ton stone slabs in Lebanon as launching strips for their space ships. Rather than being ruins of ancient temples, this visionary insisted they were monuments to the spacemen's stay on earth. As for Sodom and Gomorrah, these were destroyed in the blast-off for the spacemen's get-away from earth.

These news releases proved to be of no great consequence and presented very little problem. We took them in stride. At this point, with the successful interviews with several high officials concluded, I was prepared for almost anything.

The Rythers and I spent the latter part of the evening talking about our progress, being completely unaware that the next day would bring a thrilling development.

Suddenly the telephone rings. It is the Pasha. He informs me that His Excellency, the Prime Minister, has arranged an audience for me with the King! The average American can perhaps get an inkling of what this invitation means if he realizes how rarely the ordinary citizen of our own country can get an appointment with the President.

The Pasha says the appointment is for the following morning, so we try to prepare ourselves the rest of the evening. Miss Conway has come over from Bethlehem to see Dot and will be included in the party. The girls, of course, talk about what to wear, how to act, and what to say. They wonder if they should curtsy to the King. I tell them to practice; Dean and I will only have to bow.

The tensions begin to tell on all of us, and I get an idea. "How would you like to hear something about the background of the King?"

That does it. They arrange themselves around me and wait for the story.

"To begin with, his full name is Hussein ibn Abdullah el Hasim. His grandfather was King Abdullah and his father, King Talal. I've been around Jordan quite a few years and have seen both of them. Anyway, Hussein was the first of four children, three sons and a daughter, born to the Emir (Prince) Talal and the Hashemite Sherifa (Princess) Zain, in Amman on May 2, 1935. By our western calendar, that was November 14 of the same year. His father was deposed because of ill health when Hussein was only sixteen years old. Hussein became the King then. That was in 1953. The ceremonies took place on his birthday, and all Jordan celebrated. Amman put on a special parade. Armored cars, jeeps, and mounted troops of the Arab Legion escorted the new King. He wore the Legion's blue and gold officer's uniform and it sounded like a full-scale battle when they fired a 101 gun salute in Amman and Old Jerusalem."

By this time the others are beginning to relax. I sit down by a window and think over what I know about the youthful ruler.

His Majesty, since his ascension to the throne, has led his kingdom from near chaos to order with courage and dignity. He has steadfastly upheld the principles of freedom against forces threatening to destroy him. His people are solidly united behind him, and despite Communistic pressures from without and within, he has continued to follow a policy based on Arab unity, sovereignty, and strength.

What I knew of the King's character made me humbly appreciative of the honor he was bestowing on me in granting an audience. But he possessed other attributes which made me anxious to meet him.

The King is an avid sportsman, being a jet pilot, skier, fencer, and gifted horseman. He has become familiar with SCUBA diving, and I felt that this common interest would establish immediate rapport between us.

We went to bed anticipating the morrow.

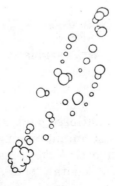

V. HIS MAJESTY, KING HUSSEIN

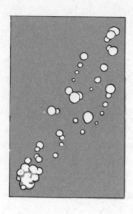

PATRONAGE BESTOWED

The morning sun peeps through the shutters, and we awaken to a day of great promise. Our appointment is at the King's Palace, and we are to be there precisely at 10:00 A.M.

I call Mike Handel, my business manager at the Christian Approach Mission, and ask him to join our party. He is flattered and comes right over. While we make last minute preparations for this all-important audience, Mike regales us with an interesting sidelight on the local scene.

"I wish you could see the excitement in Bethlehem when the government announces that the King is coming there. The Mayor always asks that all institutions and important businesses erect arches over the roads on which the King and his entourage will drive. Of course, you know there is only one main road from Jerusalem to Bethlehem. Our buildings at the Mission face that road, so we always erect arches. Mostly, the Trade School boys do the work because they have to cut pine boughs and climb the ladders over the road. We have a large crown on which we put lights from Christmas decorations, and this crown is placed in the center of the arch over the road. On the day scheduled for the King's arrival, the children are all lined up on both sides of the road in front of our buildings. Our Orphan Home Band is ready in their red and gray uniforms. They are a fine looking group all dressed in their Sunday best, waiting to applaud the King as he passes. After the royal party has passed, all the children and the boys of the band walk to Manger Square where thousands of people have gathered to pay homage to their monarch. The Orphan Home Band is always asked to play for these occasions, which naturally makes us very proud."

All the time Mike is talking, each of us is mentally rehearsing for the reception. As the time nears for us to go, I mark a red circle around February 16, 1960 on my calendar. For this meeting today may well be the most important event in setting up the actual exploration. If the King sees fit to give the project his personal blessing and patronage, the expedition will gain tremendous prestige in the eyes of the rest of the world, and I can perhaps get the equipment and personnel I need to complete my venture.

It is 9:30. We do not dare to be late, so we leave immediately. Arriving at the gates of the royal Palace, a beautiful structure of native stone situated at the top of one of Amman's "mountains", Mike waits in the car, and we are ushered into the office of the Minister of Protocol. He greets us warmly and leads us through a hall with polished gleaming floors to a reception room where we are to await our audience with His Majesty, the King.

As we sit waiting, aides to the King come in, offering us the traditional coffee and sweets and ask us about diving. As we sip the coffee from exquisite fragile cups, the Prime Minister, whom we now look upon as a friend and ally, enters the room. I am glad he is here, and I thank him for making this audience with the King possible. He replies that he is happy to be of service as he feels that King Hussein, being interested in such activities, would wish to be personally informed about our expedition. After a few more remarks, he leaves, and shortly, the Minister of Protocol steps to the door and says, simply, "Will you come now, please?"

As we pass into the private audience chambers, our names are announced one by one. His Majesty, standing just inside the doorway, greets us most graciously. We approach; Dean and I bow; the girls

take a deep breath and curtsy in elegant fashion. Fleetingly, I am pleased at their proficiency in an act unfamiliar to them. The King smiles his acknowledgement, and in well modulated tones, bids us enter.

His Majesty, the King of Jordan is a striking man because of his large dark eyes which seem to take in everything at a glance, yet reflect a kind and sensitive personality. He is of medium height, of athletic build, and wears a small mustache. Today, he is impeccably groomed in a gray tweed suit.

The room itself is luxuriously appointed with magnificent oriental rugs, Italian marble, and classical Renaissance pieces. A long couch upholstered in lustrous brocade decorates a corner. Exquisite pieces of native handicraft and artistry are on display, and a delicate bit of Bethlehem lace is exhibited under the glass top of the coffee table. The two American-made colored telephones atop His Majesty's desk bring a gleam into Dean's eyes.

Seating himself in a chair by his desk, the King gracefully waves us to the long couch at his right. He puts us at ease at once with his fluent use of English and his warm cordiality. I am pleased to find him in this receptive mood as so much depends on the general atmosphere. I can see by his expression—alert and interested—that now is the moment I have been waiting for. I take a deep breath, and say, formally,

"Your Majesty, may I say how deeply grateful we are for this audience? And may I also express my

The King looks pleased and nods his approval for me to continue.

appreciation for the kind assistance and cooperation given us by Dr. Dejani, your Director of the Department of Antiquities and also by His Excellency the Prime Minister, Hazza Majali."

The King looks pleased and nods his approval for me to continue.

"May I also give greetings to you on behalf of the many thousands of American friends of Jordan who are making the work of the Holy Land Christian Approach Mission here possible through their contributions? In America, the plight of the refugees and the need of the sick and orphans in Jordan find sympathy in our hearts. We in America have seen Your Majesty on television there, and my friends envy my opportunity to personally extend their best wishes."

With a slight nod, the King graciously acknowledges the greeting and waits for me to continue.

"As you know, Your Majesty, I have the honor to be the Director of the Mission here in Jordan. Now, I come in a different capacity, as Director of the Dead Sea Expedition. May I take a moment of Your Majesty's time to outline the purpose of this expedition?"

His Majesty leans back in his chair, folds his hands, and an intent look encourages me to go on.

"Your Majesty, although many people, especially Bible students have long been aware of the historical role and biblical significance of the Dead Sea area, until now, there has never been a scientific mapping and charting of its topography. It is my intention to do this. There have been other marine archaeological expeditions in other parts of the world, but because of its high saline content, the Dead Sea has resisted even consideration as an area for diving. Ever since 1936 when I first came to Jordan—now my second home—as a student of archaeology and oceanography, I have waited and planned for just such an opportunity. With the perfecting of many inventions related to undersea exploration, it is now possible to penetrate these poisonous waters and uncover the many secrets buried here."

During this long speech, I feel tense and watch closely for any signs that the King wishes me to stop. However, the intent look on his face appears to deepen with interest so, I lift my briefcase to my knees, extract several pictures and my working map, and continue.

"I have spent many years in research, study, and acquiring the equipment to make this expedition a success, Your Majesty. Ever since I was a boy, I have been fascinated by underwater exploration. I've even experimented with my own equipment, but that's another story, Your Majesty. Here are some pictures of the actual equipment we will use on this expedition. It was airlifted to Jordan from America, all twelve hundred pounds of it."

I hand the pictures to the King, one by one, and explain each item. He is familiar with most and as he inspects them and passes them back, I number them. Then I take the working map out to show him the locations I feel will most likely give up their secrets. He immediately notices the Prime Minister's signature and smiles.

All during my monologue, the King has not spoken, but now his questions reveal a keen interest in and an intimate knowledge of diving equipment and procedures. To his queries on the potentialities of the expedition, I hasten to reply,

"Your Majesty, I have consulted leading world archaeologists to get as good advice as I could concerning these historical sites. Now if I can get certain equipment and personnel I need, here in Jordan, there is no reason the expedition should not be successful. I am convinced that the lost cities are there; I intend to bring up evidence of them."

The King appears to be lost in thought for a moment. I exchange anxious glances with Dean; the girls sit stiffly at their end of the couch. The success of our project may well hinge on the next few moments.

The King seems to become aware of the momentary silence, smiles gently in understanding, and to our relief, asks me to explain just what our procedures will be.

"Well, Your Majesty, first we will chart the topography of the sea bottom of the likeliest areas from the deck of the boat. Then, if the Sonar equipment shows any irregularities, Mr. Ryther and I will go down and explore in the area. After this comes the coring. The cores will then be evaluated by eminent scientists, and any artifacts found will be announced to the world. After the coring operation, we intend to go down and photograph, if we can, the entire location. Ultimately I hope to excavate any remnants of the lost cities we find. I know, Your Majesty, that this is a simplification of what we are setting out to do, but I will be honored to answer any question in detail you may care to pose."

The King seems extremely interested in the coring and mapping operations, asks several penetrating questions, seems satisfied with my answers and then wants to know how the expedition can prove beneficial to his kingdom.

"Your Majesty, I am convinced that not only will we find the lost cities but also evidences of other lost historical civilizations under the Dead Sea. Think what this can mean to Jordan. Other archaeological expeditions will follow and piece together a living story of the Jordan that was, how importantly it figured in the story of the Bible, and how today it is linked in greatness to past glories. All the world will know and revere your kingdom, Your Majesty!"

The King receives my discourse in silence, but the look on his face belies his calm. I can see he is analyzing the potentiality of the contribution which this expedition could possibly make.

From this moment on, it is apparent my adventure has captured the King's imagination, and we are encouraged to think he will provide help in the undertaking. He asks in what way he can be of help. This is my cue.

"After setting up the expedition, and reaching Jordan, Your Majesty, I find that financially and through pressure of time, I will be unable to proceed without some practical assistance. It is my hope and prayer, Your Majesty, that if you find this outline of my proposal acceptable, you might place the expedition under your patronage."

He listens gravely to my plea and then asks what specific assistance I will need.

"Your Majesty, we will need boats, aircraft, and competent personnel. We cannot build our own boat big enough to house the Sonar and diving equipment; perhaps your Navy can lend us one. And if your Air Force can let us have a stand-by plane . . . We'll need that as well as a helicopter in case Mr. Ryther or I need immediate transportation to a decompression chamber. It is possible there may be a malfunction of diving equipment or some other unforeseen accident, and the nearest decompression chamber is on board a ship of the U.S. fleet in the Mediterranean on maneuvers. As you know, time is of the essence in such circumstances as these."

The King mulls over my reply for just a moment then states he is extremely interested in the expedition and is sure he can put the Armed Forces, with the needed equipment, at our disposal. He then asks if we can arrange to return the next day for a conference with his chiefs of the Armed Forces. Immediately I answer,

"I am at your command, Your Majesty!"

At this, the King rises; we follow suit. The audience is over. Solemnly, he shakes our hands and bids us good-bye. We leave the room passing between the two gigantic Russian Cossack costumed guards at the door and walk, a least a foot off the ground, to the car where Mike is waiting. As we get in, Mike looks at his watch and shakes his head in disbelief. We have been closeted with the King long past the usual short time allotted for interviews.

On the drive back, no one speaks. It is not until we are seated at the lunch table in the Philadelphia Hotel that the full impact strikes Dean and the girls. Mike breaks the silence with, "Come on now, don't sit there speechless. Tell me how our King was impressed with your plans."

Dot excitedly tells him about the interview and its encouraging outcome.

Mike beams at the good news. I congratulate Dean, Dot and Vi on their behavior in the Royal presence, then Dean says, "Meeting the King is worth the whole trip to Jordan, even if I never get to dive in the Dead Sea at all. But have you considered? Here we are, everybody knows us. It's common knowledge the King has granted us an audience. And so far we haven't wet a fin! Supposing when we dive, we come up empty-handed? What then?"

"Why Dean, I don't see how we can miss." I turn to face him directly as I speak. "Two of our biggest problems have just been solved. We thought we'd have to build our own boat; that's been taken care of, thanks to the Jordan Navy, so the charting

71

and mapping of the Dead Sea should be accomplished without too much difficulty. And the stand-by plane takes another worry off our minds. No sir, Dean, you just navigate the boat so we don't drift; Dot, you transcribe the sonar readings on the chart; then Dean, you and I go to the bottom to explore and I don't think we need worry about the expedition being successful. I'm sure we'll find the lost cities."

"Well, after today, Dr. Baney, with the King giving us his blessing and assistance," says Dean, "I believe I would be willing to go down deeper and stay there longer just for his sake. You can count on me."

"Just don't forget to come up," commands Dot.

"There won't be any mermaids sitting on rocks at the bottom of this Sea, my dear, so don't worry. I don't have any intention of staying down too long and being pickled in Dead Sea water," retorts Dean.

Mike sits listening, but he does not see anything humorous in our remarks. He continues to believe we are courting doom every time we don mask and flippers to go beneath those waters until the day we take them off for the last time on the shores of the Dead Sea.

Later that day, Dean and I get down to some serious planning and discussion, with Mike in on the conference as advisor on the availability of such things as lead weights, which we are going to have to find in Amman to complete our diving gear.

We decide that we will have to wear a considerable amount of extra lead to give us a neutral buoyancy in the water. We have calculated that the pressures of this water will be far more intense than those in other seas. For instance, at a depth of thirty feet in the Dead Sea, pressure would be equal to a depth of perhaps fifty feet in ordinary sea water. The high rate of evaporation in this greatest geographic depression in the world accounts for the extreme salinity of the water. This is about twenty-five per cent as compared with only four to six percent in ordinary sea water. A contributing factor to the saltiness is that there is no outlet to the Dead Sea. With this in mind, we decided that, for safety purposes, we should test all our equipment in a normal sea before risking possible malfunction in the "Sea of Death". We reason that if the equipment doesn't work properly in ordinary sea water, it won't function in the Dead Sea.

The nearest sea water is the Mediterranean at Beirut and the Red Sea at Akaba, at the extreme southern tip of Jordan. Since Dean and I have already dived into the Mediterranean, we choose the Red Sea to check out our equipment.

Our twelve hundred pounds of equipment demands the use of a small truck besides a car. This is one of several problems created by our decision to pre-test in the Red Sea. Dean brings up the need for a stand-by 'plane at Akaba.

"We're talking about testing the equipment to a depth in excess of 200 feet. Dr. Baney don't you think we'd better make some arrangements to get to a decompression chamber in a hurry in case something goes wrong. We can't take a chance out here on one of us getting paralysis of the depths, or worse!"

I agree on the necessity for a stand-by 'plane.

Mike is called to the telephone about this time and comes back with the message that our equipment has arrived and is being taken to the Pasha's warehouse for clearance through customs. This is good news as we have been waiting for it eagerly. After a few more comments on the proposed dive into the Red Sea, we retire for the night.

The next morning at eleven o'clock, word comes from Dr. Dejani that the Protocol office of the Royal Palace has telephoned. His Majesty requests our presence at 12:30.

Dean and I get ready, and Mike drives us to the office of Dr. Dejani who accompanies us to the Palace. On the way, he informs us that he is soon to make a trip to the United States and will be gone for six months. We are sorry to hear of his leaving. The acting Director will be a Mr. Diya Rafieh.

On arriving, we are again shown into the reception hall where we are introduced to a number of distinguished gentlemen, the commanders of His Majesty's Armed Forces. They are the Commanders-in-chief of the Army and Navy, the Chiefs of the Jordanian Air Force, and the Director of Tourism whom I already knew. The Prime Minister is also there.

In a few moments, all of us are ushered into His Majesty's reception room, and we pay our respects. His Majesty requests me to outline the procedures I intend to follow for the benefit of his commanders. I tell them of my plan to map and chart the northern end of the Dead Sea around the Khirbet Qumran area where the Dead Sea Scrolls were found, and then repeat this operation in the Lisan area. Mrs. Ryther, our technical assistant, will keep detailed maps and charts of these areas as we cover them. They seem pleased with this plan since this had never been done before in the Dead Sea.

They ask me what facilities the expedition will require, and I repeat what I had told the King the previous day; that we could use the cooperation and facilities of the Jordan Army, Navy, and Air Force to transport ourselves and our equipment on land, on the water, and in the air. We would also need the assistance of qualified personnel. With all this help, I believed we would make a valuable contribution to Jordan. I then tell them of my intention to test our all-new equipment in the Red Sea at Akaba. They understand I will need a stand-by plane there as well as our transportation to and from Akaba.

There is a short discussion between His Majesty and his Commanders and in the end, they inform me they are very enthusiastic about carrying out His Majesty's request that I be furnished all the equipment and personnel I will require. I express my gratitude to His Majesty for placing our expedition under his patronage and for extending to us these much-needed services. I tell him we will give our best in energy and determination to making the expedition a success. He very graciously repeats his confidence in our ability to make the expedition a success, and, after the formalities are observed, this second audience comes to an end.

In the anteroom after leaving the King's chambers, the Commander of the Army shakes my hand and says, "Dr. Baney, you are to be congratulated. His Majesty has shown extreme interest in your expedition by requesting the necessary equipment be put at your disposal."

I agree that I have indeed been fortunate. Dr. Dejani invites Dean and me to lunch with him, and we leave the Palace. At lunch, I thank Dr. Dejani again for his excellent cooperation and wish him a pleasant time on his forthcoming trip to the United States.

Dean and I return to the hotel and plan for the testing of our equipment in the Red Sea at Akaba.

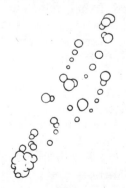

VI.   THE RED SEA

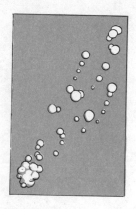

(TESTING IN DEPTHS WHERE FATE IS THE HUNTER)

The following morning Dean and I start on the arrangements to move sixty items of equipment and ourselves to the Akaba area. We call on the Chief of the Army, Brigadier General Abdullah Majalli at Army headquarters here in Amman to procure the stand-by plane he had promised the previous day.

He is pleased to see us and suggests I list our needs for each different operational stage with his office. As for the stand-by plane, the General has it ready.

"I would like to complete the testing of our equipment as quickly as possible," I tell him. "Could we leave as early as eight o'clock tomorrow morning for Akaba?"

General Majalli says the necessary arrangements will be made and adds, as we leave, that he is sure the expedition will be successful especially since we have His Majesty's endorsement.

There will be seven of us making the trip to the Red Sea. Mike Handel will be our leading 'tenderman'; he has been training young Naim Shaer as his assistant. Naim has been an ambulance driver of our mobile medical clinic at the mission for some years and is a willing worker.

In addition, our party has been joined by a Mr. Flouty, the Royal photographer by appointment. He came to our hotel waving a cablegram he had received from the Associated Press in New York, asking him to give this expedition, complete coverage including the testing of equipment at Akaba. Movie-Tone News also wanted some footage. Mr. Flouty turned out to be not only a good photographer, but also a good traveling companion and helpful in many ways.

We are going to Akaba to rigorously test every bit of the equipment and apparatus in dive after dive until we are convinced each is trustworthy. We will be diving in the Dead Sea for almost three months and cannot risk the smallest defect in our gear.

At the airport the next morning there are two planes waiting, one twin engine and one four-engine. With our equipment weighing over 1,000 pounds plus the combined weight of us seven, the pilot decides on the four-engine DeHaviland, used privately by the King when he is not flying a jet. The pilot is King Hussein's private pilot.

The flight takes about an hour and is very enjoyable. The morning is clear and warm, and visibility is perfect. From Amman we fly a south-westerly course, crossing the Moab Mountains to the Dead Sea, then following the eastern shoreline. For a considerable distance, perhaps twenty to thirty miles, the red Nubian sandstone cliffs rise like a sheer wall from the depths of the sea. Some of these mountain peaks are virtually inaccessible by foot. Our pilot points out various landmarks such as the Macaerus peak, soaring 3,000 feet over the Dead Sea abyss, and the Arnon River, largest of the few streams that pass through narrow gorges from the plateau of the Moab country to reach the Dead Sea. From a distance, the "violet" mountains of Moab look as though they have been painted in pastel colors with a palette knife on the landscape below us. The clefts in the rock and deep valleys are purple shadows as the sun hits the mountains at an angle. Only one road winds north and south. As we near the Lisan peninsula area, the mountains recede as we come upon green plains watered by tiny streams. Here is the 'tongue' protruding its pallid tip into the blue waters of the Sea. We expect to become very familiar with this whole area as it will be one of our bases of operation.

There is a long stretch of withered mountainous desert before our plane began approaching Akaba. The pilot circles the city several times to allow Mr. Flouty enough time to take several aerial shots of the area. After landing, other photographs are taken of the plane, members of the party, and the equipment being unloaded.

Another plane is arriving. "What is this plane coming in?" I ask our pilot.

"That is your stand-by plane", he says. "This one must return to Amman as soon as it is unloaded."

The twin engine plane has been flown here for our use during our stay in Akaba. We also find a jeep at our disposal, complete with driver.

We climb into the jeep and jolt along the road to the Akaba Rest House, a small but comfortable hostel right on the sandy beach. It also has a beach house within fifteen feet of the sea where we unpack our crates of diving equipment.

For years, Akaba has been a quiet seaside fishing village, at the edge of a desert wilderness tucked away between large mountain ranges. Because of its isolated location at the northernmost point of the Red Sea, large sea going vessels formerly had not stopped there. Now, Akaba is a busy, fast-growing harbor city, handling considerable import and export trade.

A new road, following the ancient highway built by the Romans, has just been opened from here to the capitol city (Amman), and Akaba with its perfect winter-time climate, its serene beauty, and its proximity to the Red Sea, should become a tourist attraction in the not too distant future. Akaba, with its colorful, inspiring mountain backdrop, sandy beaches, and lovely clear blue water of the Red Sea at its doorstep is picturesque. When it is modernized, Akaba will be a bustling winter resort. There will be first-class hotels, restaurants, sailing and water sports, including, of course, the scuba diving we were now introducing.

"Dr. Baney, let's have the boys unpack the cases so we can dive before lunch," Dean calls to me from the beach house. "O.K.", I answer and go to my room to put on swim trunks. Then I hurry to the beach where Dean, Mike and Naim are removing equipment and gear from the large cases. Soon everything is unpacked and assembled ready for use. We choose the articles we want to test first.

Although our arrival had not been announced, it is not long before a number of spectators have gathered to watch us. The more curious keep pointing at first to one item then another, laid out on the red-checkered tablecloths we had spread on the sand.

"Ish hadda?" (what is this), they ask. I have Mike answer all questions on how this motley assortment of gear will take us under water and allow us to breathe.

Dot is checking our gear against her inventory sheet as it is unpacked while Dean and I are getting into our neoprene rubber diving suits. "You know what Mike is telling these boys?" she calls out, "He's saying your yellow suits are to scare the sharks and whales away!"

Not long after this, I overheard Naim telling one of the police lieutenants in the crowd that our big air tanks are to keep us from going down too deep! Our tendermen are really coloring the facts, but I don't want to take the time just then for a lecture on scuba diving and its related equipment, so I let my Jordanians go on, and we continued gearing up. Meanwhile, Mr. Flouty is busy taking pictures of our equipment and gets several good shots of our two underwater propulsion devices, the Sea Shark and the Sea-Tow Minnow.

These pieces fascinated the Akaba citizens. The Sea-Tow Minnow, especially, with its torpedo-like body and propeller, was quite unique in their eyes. Later, when we tested these pieces, the onlookers would 'ooh' and 'ah' at the spectacle. After our tendermen helped lift them into the water, it was an awesome sight to see us disappear with them at one point under the waves and then in a few seconds come shooting up some distance away. Under test conditions, the two propulsion pieces functioned perfectly.

The only difficulty we had with them later was in weighting them for practical use in the Dead Sea.

Once outfitted, we decided to test some of the smaller items first: the depth gauges, underwater watches and compasses, masks and regulators. We especially want to make sure of our large number of regulators. This is the most important piece of equipment a diver uses. Actually it is his 'lung'. The regulator equalizes the pressures on the outside with the inner pressures, and keeps the diver breathing naturally. Since these are so important, we intend to take one set down, return for another, dive again, and repeat this procedure until we are fully confident of their worthiness.

On our first dive, we also take our spear guns as we have been told there are sharks around here.

We have carefully chosen where we will dive, believing we will find a gradual decline of the sea floor rather than a drop-off. After a final check, we walk into the sea, much to the amusement and amazement of our audience. Dean and I descended cautiously, close together, intending to stay down for one hour unless the equipment fails to function properly.

"Come up every few minutes and let us know you are all right," sings out Mike as we go under, and I suddenly imagine Dean and me bobbing up and down like corks, waving at the crowd on the beach.

"Bring me back a chest of gold," calls out Naim.

We find that to achieve neutral buoyancy we are forced to carry eighteen pounds of weights on our belts. After going down about 25 feet, Dean gives the signal to ascend, and we start upward. Surfacing, he explains that his new mask is not sealing to his face, letting water inside. We check but can find no reason for the malfunction and go down again. Dean cannot keep the water out of the mask, however, so we surface again to exchange it for another. The defective one is marked by Dot as unusable; Dean takes a new one, and we descend again into the blue loneliness. This one fits perfectly.

At 40 feet we pause and rest on the bottom to check our bearings and equipment. Everything is

working perfectly. We look around us and find we are sitting in the middle of what looks like an underwater hay field. The visibility is so good that we can see clearly for almost a thousand yards in every direction. If I'd had one, I could easily have read a small-print newspaper in this clear sun-brightened spot.

All around us the sea-grass stands from one to two feet high, waving lazily to and fro. The scene looks like a hay field on a Missouri farm. There are hundreds of different types of fish; some we recognize, some are unfamiliar. I see one called the 'sea hare' because of its long antennae which look like ears. I decided not to shoot it as rabbit season is over in Missouri.

Traveling on we became aware that the sea floor is gradually lowering. This we can tell by our depth gauges and quite often by the functioning of our regulators. At depths below 100 feet the diver may have difficulty in judging whether the sea bed is level or sloping. He has the illusion that the bottom is level; only a glance at his depth gauge orients him. It is not unusual for a diver to descend 25 feet on an incline in a distance of 50-100 feet without being aware of it.

We pass over the "hay field" with its multitude of "farm animals" as I call them. The scenery changes, and the sea floor is now white sand. At a depth of 75 feet, we approach a magnificent world of fantasy: unbelievably exquisite coral formations. Finding a convenient spot, we rest our knees on the sand and begin checking our gear. We take our bearings and finding the instruments functioning properly, swim on around large bluffs of coral. We seem to be following a path of white sand winding between two bluffs. The sea around teems with vari-colored fish ignoring our intrusion into their world.

We soon reach a depth of 110 feet, and we again pause, just above the bluffs, to re-check each other's equipment. In underwater sign language, Dean motions that all his gear is O.K. and I do likewise. On checking our watches and depth gauges, however, we discover that we have used up far more time and air than we had realized and have only 25 more minutes remaining until time to surface.

Swimming on, we come to an area which has apparently been good fishing grounds. There are a number of discarded nets, some the native basket-type. One net is still usable; a cable has become disconnected and the net lost. The trap still has bait in it, but no fish. Also, various objects, discarded or dropped from the ships in the harbor litter the sea-floor here. There are anchors, tangled ropes, and other items — nothing worth salvaging. Our next check point is at the 143 foot mark. We descend still farther, following our path of white sand. We find ourselves in an enormous subterranean forest of shrubs, and boulders—the forest of my "Missouri farm". The beauty and clarity of the water is astounding. I want to sit there and watch this fascinating sea-scape with its multitude of fish.

Various types of coral abound here. Besides the solid reefs, there are many large, round boulders, known as Brain corals and Gonipora. The Porites look like cabbages, and staghorns, delicate for coral, and the red Mediterranean coral from which jewelry is made dazzle the eye. We try not to scrape against any of them as the coral points are sharp, and some are poisonous.

Mr. Flouty had asked us to bring up a shark for him to photograph, but our new French-made spear guns find no target here. Time is fleeting, and since we still must pause during the ascent to decompress, we start for the surface. Instead of rising directly, we travel back over the "hay field" or "farm". This time our scant air supply prevents our stopping.

When we have surfaced and swam back to the beach, we are met by Mike and Naim running through the surf. Both are agitated. "We thought you had drowned. What happened? Why were you down so long?" Words spill from them in their anxiety. We calm them down, and they can see we are all right. The exertion of helping us take off our gear returns them to normal. Mike is soon passing out exclusive bits of information to the onlookers.

After we change into street clothes, we all go to the cafe in the Rest House where we meet many people wanting to know more about diving.

The Governor of the Akaba district and the Chief of Police with a number of his lieutenants invite us to lunch with them. Diving is an altogether new topic of conversation, and they listen raptly as Dean and I discuss our morning dive. The new pieces of equipment have passed the test with the exception of that one mask. We decide that equipment which can work properly at 143 feet can surely function all right at half that depth in the Dead Sea.

Talking about my "Missouri farm" at the bottom of the Red Sea causes quite a stir among the listeners.

"You saw cows and pigs and chickens walking in the Sea?" asks one of them, taking me seriously. Everyone looks doubtful, so I stretch the joke as far as I can, describing animals feeding in the meadow, and the "hare" which I didn't shoot because the season for shooting rabbits was over.

The Governor is not taken in, however. "This is Jordan, so you should have seen some camels grazing in that pasture, and did you see a turkey fish?" he asks.

Now the Governor has one on me for I had forgotten to say anything about camels on the farm, and we had not sighted a single turkey fish this morning. I tell the Governor that raising turkeys is a specialized business in Missouri and this particular farm does not happen to have a single turkey on it. "But on my next dive I will bring you back a turkey," I tell him.

"Oh no, leave them alone," he warns. "We want you to enjoy your stay with us in Akaba and not be poisoned. Please stick to your Missouri variety of turkeys and let the Red Sea turkeys alone."

The others around the table are curious, so I explain that the turkey fish, or "lion fish" as it is called in other parts of the world, is one of the most beautiful yet most deadly of the fish which inhabit the coral reefs. It is covered with gorgeous "feathers." The fins and the tail are ruffled like the petals of a flower. It has long, sharp poisonous spines raised on its back ridge which can inflict most painful wounds.

"Sharks, snakes, barracuda, deadly turkey fish, poison coral, sting rays! Even the desire to see your underwater Missouri farm cannot make me dive into these waters, Dr. Baney!" And Mike shakes his head as he gets up to call the waiter for our coffee.

After lunch we observe the custom of the country and take a siesta before starting on our afternoon dive to test more equipment. This afternoon we plan to test our double tank blocks and other new equipment at even greater depths.

Dean vetoes the idea of covering the same territory as too much time and air will be wasted. Reluctantly I agree to enter the sea from a different area where we can reach deeper water closer to shore. We again take our spear guns but not for checking out since there is no living thing in the Dead Sea.

At the bottom we pause, resting one knee in the sand, check each other's equipment, and further plot our course. By the time we reach 100 feet we are in an area abundant with coral and cannot find a sandy spot on which to rest. The coral formations are needle sharp and can easily rip a fin or tear the skin. When it is necessary to check our equipment, we pause suspended just above it if we can, or if not, step very gingerly on a solid piece.

At this depth, Dean and I keep close together and keep looking into each other's face masks. We are alert to any signs of unusual behavior, indicating nitrogen narcosis, the dread "rapture of the depths" all divers fear. At any depth below 140 feet, nitrogen may build up in the diver's body and drug his senses. All divers fear it; some have fallen prey to it. Those it does affect, become lightheaded and irrational, cannot concentrate, and are happily and dangerously oblivious to their plight. They might try to imitate the fish, take out their mouthpieces and drown.

Farther on, we notice a very large ship's anchor and coils of rope and cable which apparently had fallen from the ship when the anchor had been lost. The anchor is encrusted with coral and looks like an artist's conception of a surrealistic sea-scape. Swimming leisurely, we come upon another abrupt drop in the sea floor. Still we see nothing but coral around us. The visibility, at this time of day, is unlimited. The sunlight filtering down glances off the darting iridescent fish, making weird patterns of light and shadow on the coral and the brilliantly colored invertebrates which inhabit the reefs.

Going down into this abyss, Dean and I look for a trace of the white sandy path we had followed in the morning so we could sit or at least get one knee down to check our equipment.

Instead, Dean is attracted by an object about 50 feet away and wanders lazily toward it. Odd, I think. We are supposed to stay close together. I wonder if Dean is experiencing a touch of 'rapture of the deep'. I start after him as I can see him bending over the object. He has come across an old anchor, square shaped, and completely unlike any modern type. I recalled seeing pictures of similar anchors in archaeological books; this one must be 300-500 years old!

Just to make sure Dean is all right, I look directly into his eyes to see if anything is wrong. His gaze is steady, however, and I am relieved.

We float at this level for awhile as Dean inspects the anchor, when I spy an odd-shaped piece of coral about a city block away. On closer examination, I am surprised to see its resemblance to a throne, even to the armrests and high, ornately carved back. It looks so real, I can almost imagine Poseidon holding court in it. Glints of pseudo-jewels emanate from the legs as though emeralds and rubies had been embedded there as befits a royal chair. The piece is really coral although the illusion is complete. I wish that somehow we could take it with us to the surface but soon discard this impractical thought. For the past few minutes, I have felt that my buoyancy was not quite right. I am having to exert myself considerably to keep descending.

At 160 feet we stop on a comparatively smooth stretch of coral, and I notice my regulator makes more noise than is normal. I point this out to Dean. He signals he will keep constant watch for a more serious malfunction. If this should happen, he will supply me with air, sharing his own mouthpiece until we can surface.

About 60 feet below is a patch of sand. We swim side by side to a depth of 220 feet where we can rest on the sand while checking our gear and equipment. We calculate there are still 45 minutes of diving time left before we have to surface.

I am beginning to feel quite tired, however, and wonder if it is the lack of neutral buoyancy, as I am struggling to keep from rising. Besides, we have been in the water for over an hour and swimming rather hard. Resting here, I am forced to hold onto a rock to stay on the bottom, but I want to find out why I'm so tired—whether it's natural fatigue or a malfunction of my breathing apparatus. In a short time I realize it is becoming still more difficult to breathe; I have to exert all my strength to pull enough air from my mouthpiece and regulator. I immediately signal Dean to surface, and we rise together, swimming in the direction of the shore. My decision is right; as we continue the ascent I find my regulator giving me more and more trouble. I pull my relief valve but to no avail.

Dean senses my distress and keeps his eyes glued to mine. At 50 feet from the surface we halt to decompress. I am finding it almost impossible to breathe, so I motion Dean to keep going closer to the surface. Should my regulator give out completely, I can drop my weight belts, and borrow his mouthpiece until we decompress. At 20 feet, Dean gives me the much-needed air, and we continue, surfacing about a quarter-mile from shore. I gulp in huge mouthfuls of deliciously warm air, clinging to Dean for several minutes until the dizziness subsides, and I regain strength enough to swim up to the beach.

"I am so tired," I tell Dean, "it must be because I used up too much strength trying to suck in air from the defective regulator."

We have surfaced and swam back to the beach some distance from the entering point, but our watchful tendermen have spotted us. Piling into the jeep, they speed across the sand to where we are resting against the hulk of a grounded fishing boat.

"Well, where are the camels and goats?" they chorus. Their faces show their disappointment when they learn we have not brought up a single specimen after all the time we had been down. Dean explains that my regulator had kept us from going to the farm, and I console them with a promise to bring back some livestock on another occasion.

I am glad they have brought the jeep to pick us up as I am very tired. We ungear and call it a day, going back to the Rest House where I drink a quart of orange juice to regain my strength while lying on the beach soaking up the hot sun.

This dive proved to be more valuable in testing than the morning dive, in that the regulator, our most vital piece of equipment, had shown some deficiency which was intensified with the pressures of the greater depths. After checking our tanks, we determined that it was definitely the regulator causing the trouble, so we discarded it along with the defective mask. Dot marked it unsafe and not to be used in the Dead Sea.

After a short rest, Dean went back with a single tank to visit my farm under the sea. Mike and the others have been urging him to bring back "even a small goat—even a baby camel!"

Forty minutes later he surfaced with a good-sized black and yellow fish he had speared to show them. By now, everyone except Mike, wanted to learn to dive, but we had more serious business to attend to and kept telling them—Arabic fashion—

"Bah den bookrah" (Later on—tomorrow).

But on the next day, there is no time for teaching. We have come here to test equipment, and test it we do. Dive after dive with every piece finally verifies their sea-worthiness and our mission here is finally accomplished. We are ready for the main bout in the big arena, the Dead Sea.

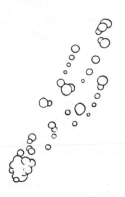

Underwater color pictures on the following pages were made as Dean and I explored the coral bluffs along the sandy pathway 150 to 200 feet below the surface of the Red Sea at Akaba, Jordan.

These pictures were made only for the purpose of testing our underwater cameras—the Leica Torpedo and the 16mm Nautilus Torpedo movie camera which had been supplied us by their inventor, Dimitri Rebikoff, in Cannes, France. No effort was made to attain any professional artistry in shooting these films. However, I believe they will serve to amplify my description of the fantastic sea creatures and beautiful coral formations we found in these cobalt blue, crystal clear waters.

The picture of me holding a "sea snake" was unposed! I saw it slithering around a coral boulder, pulled it free, then turned to Dean, motioning for him to swim over for a closer look. Instead, Dean snapped the picture, then helped me to maneuver the writhing snake into our specimen bag which we filled with many varieties of marine life and brought to the surface for examination.

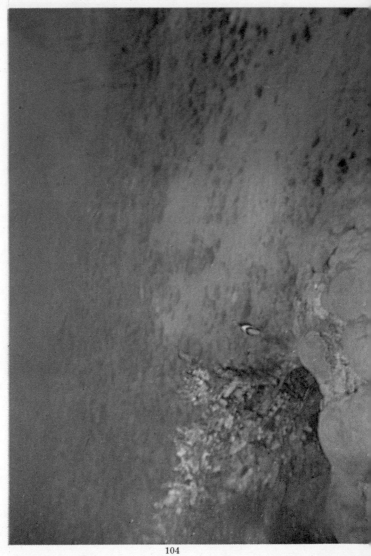

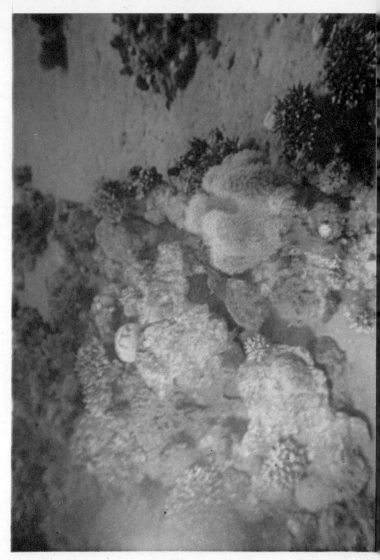

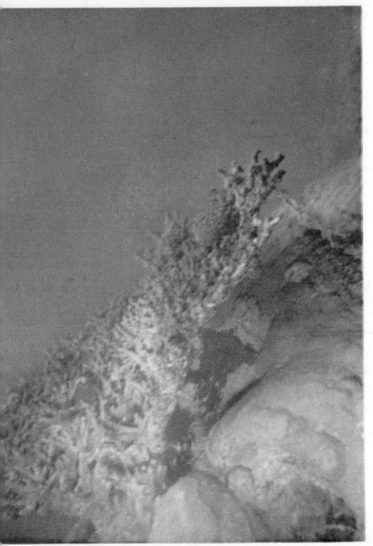

VII.   RECONNAISSANCE

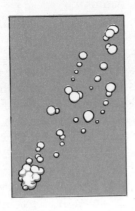

OVER ROMAN PATHWAYS TO THE LISAN PENINSULA

After our exciting experiences in Akaba, we are anxious to get started with the work in the Dead Sea. On the return trip from Akaba we had discussed some of the requirements for the boat and personnel which were to be supplied by the Royal Jordan Navy for our use during the expedition. Also, we had decided to make a trip by car to the Lisan peninsula to scout the area for possible locations for establishing a base of operations somewhere along the shore.

This may be on shore or aboard the Naval craft, we will agree on this later.   The last town of any size before the turn from the main road onto the one-lane track leading to the peninsula is Karak, 133 miles from Amman.

Dean and Dot, Mike Handel, Vi Conway, and I leave Amman in the Mission's car about 9:30 one morning in mid-February. The first couple of hours we pass many little villages. Everywhere, people are industriously working in the fields, plowing and planting. The unusual plow teams of camels and oxen together are strange—to our western eyes. Guards watch over the fields, and every few kilometers there are police posts with sentries patrolling this main artery reaching from Akaba to Amman, and all the way to Damascus in Syria. We can visualize Caesar's soldiers driving slaves into paving this first road, sections of which still exist and are used.

Soon we cross the first of the mountain ranges. The road is still good black-top, although narrow and with many sharp curves. Ahead of us and down the southern slope, the green valley stretches. We pass through all too soon, the next range of mountains has a narrower gravel road. We close our eyes as we round curve after curve, hoping neither an oncoming car nor loose gravel will force us to the edge since there are no rails here.

In three hours we reach Karak, whose square buff-colored buildings perch like a diadem on the crest of a high hill. At the port of entry we must give our names, nationalities, and occupations and here are told to proceed to the police post in the center of the town. Here, the chief of police gives us permission to proceed and assigns an armed

110

guard to guide us to our next stop. This turns out to be an Italian hospital. We are met by a Sister who arranges to put us up for the night if it is too late to return to Amman after investigating possible camp sites on the shores of the Dead Sea at the peninsula. After coffee, our policeman escort guides us out of Karak, and we head down the mountain.

This is the most hair-raising part of the trip. The road becomes narrower and more winding as we go. We can see the blue of the Dead Sea far below. It appears far, far away. Suddenly, around a curve, with brakes squealing and gravel skipping under the wheels, we come upon a jeep stalled in the middle of the road. Just in time we stop. The driver, an Englishman working for the Phillips Petroleum Company, is out here to make gravity surveys. His crew moves the jeep to the side, so we can pass.

The scenery is breath-taking. The rock formations of the mountains attest to the massive volcanic activity in this area. The whole of the Jordan valley is a great rift or geological fault caused by cataclysmic upheavals. Gigantic slabs stand on end, and whole mountains of basalt lay on a slant. In the crevice grow wild flowers of all colors and description, and in the valley we are rapidly approaching, are fields which resemble oriental carpets, so profusely are they blanketed with spring blossoms.

We have turned off the main road by now and are traveling west on the valley floor, passing

many Bedouin encampments with their tomato and potato fields. Our car has a tough task fording the irrigation streams crossing the road at intervals. Sometimes we have to get out and walk to lighten the load so the oil pan won't scrape the road. Dean and I agree this trip cannot be made every day by car, even for mail and supplies, if we are to base our camp on these shores while diving in the southern section of the Dead Sea.

After a good many bone-rattling miles, we arrive at the beach which is far from promising as a site for the camp. There is no sand—only rock, gravel, and mud. We get out of the car to survey the location and get our bearings. A clump of tamarisk trees provide shade, and the girls set out the lunch which the hotel had packed that morning. Right now, nothing tastes better than the long hardcrusted rolls slit in the center, filled with cheese, sardines, and hard boiled eggs. We use our water sparingly to wash these down.

While we eat, our police escort goes to visit some of the Bedouins nearby. They bring over a crate of the largest tomatoes we have ever seen along with green peppers for their friend, the policeman. We sample the vegetables after washing them carefully. They are as delicious as they look.

An audience gathers as usual. When we finish eating, Mike asks one of the boys to walk out into the water in various spots. Dean and I have not brought any diving gear this trip, but we want to get an idea about the type of bottom along the shore line. We follow the boy and discover the shore bottom is gravel.

Back in the car, we follow a camel track along the sun-baked ground as far south as we can go. At the end of the trail are a number of Bedouin tents with crowds of children milling about. The children, unused to seeing strangers in this out-of-the way place peer curiously at us, especially at the girls. Vi tries to make friends, practicing her Arabic, but they only giggle, cover their faces with their hands and run back to the tents. Dot and Vi stay in the car while Dean, Mike and I test the bottom of the Dead Sea shoreline at this point.

This place must have been a trading site in the past for there are two fairly large boats rotting at the water's edge. We are told they have not been used for years but that at one time they were loaded with vegetables and sailed across to Jericho at the northern end of the Dead Sea.

The beach here is not gravel but mud, and the water is very shallow for a considerable distance.

Escaping the crowd of curious children, we drive to a nearby village where our police escort radios the Karak post from a National Guard station. We find we have been expected here and arrangements have been made for us to stay all night in one of the houses. I decide we should return to Amman and not stay.

It is getting dark as we reach Karak. Our police escort retrieves his basket of tomatoes, tips his cap, and leaves. We proceed to the Italian Hospital to replenish our water supply and to tell the good Sister we will continue to Amman.

Everywhere along the way the people with whom we talked were most congenial and anxious to help. Their hospitality was beyond measure. Their possessions might have been few, but they would have shared them with us gladly. The Arabic for "you are welcome" is "Ahlan Wasahlan," and these people really mean it when you are invited to cross their threshold or to share their bread and salt.

At 9:30 that night, we made it back to the comparative comfort of our rooms at the hotel, a tired, bedraggled group after a rough day.

VIII.   BULLETS

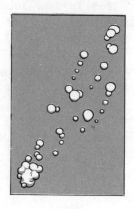

SHOOT US DOWN TO THE SEA'S BURIED SECRETS

Though our trip to Lisan had not been too profitable in terms of an exact location for a base camp, still, valuable knowledge of the terrain had been gained. The scouting out of the way, now the serious business of outfitting the boats and testing the weights in the Dead Sea itself became the next order of business on our schedule.

We are going to the Mission the next day and will take a side trip to the harbor on the way. The harbor is located at the northern end of the Dead Sea only a few miles from the main road. Leaving Amman, we travel the new road which by-passes Jericho but joins the Jericho-Jerusalem road just before it begins its laborious climb through the

Judean mountains from the valley floor, which is 700 feet below sea level, to Jerusalem, 2,593 feet above sea level. Nearing the Jordan River, we come upon the "quattara"—eroded desert land of queer-shaped mounds formed by the winds and cutting edges of sand through the centuries. The earth here is soft and spongy, covered with gypsum and salt which crumbles underfoot.

Turning onto a side road leading to the Dead Sea, Mike stops the car to let a herd of camels cross the road. There are a number of baby camels in it. When the last little fellow has struggled across, Mike "back-fires" the car, sending the skittish youngsters racing to their mothers, and we speed down the road to the harbor.

Mike stops the car as we come to the gate of the port authority. This is the first and only time we are required to stop because from then on the guards recognize us and open the gate when they see the car approaching. Mike parks in front of the headquarters building. The captain bids us welcome, and according to custom, offers us coffee. Then we walk to the pier to look over the boats which have been assigned to us. "The big one is about forty feet long and nine feet wide", says the captain. "Four people can sleep on this boat." It looks quite sturdy.

"Hadda quais?" (This is good?) asks the captain. "Quais kateer" (very good), I reply. But on closer inspection I realize there will be many modifications to be made before this boat is fully equipped for the job ahead.

All the way to Bethlehem we make plans to fit out the big boat to suit our requirements for diving, and to make it comfortable to spend long days and nights aboard while charting the topography of the Sea, making exploratory dives, and working long distances from home base—the Navy harbor. Of the three assigned, two are cruisers and one a landing craft, used as patrol boats to watch over the borders and sea shores, they are hardly adequate as they are, for the expedition.

Alterations will have to be made in the larger cruiser for the installation of the Sonar equipment, coring devices, and the set up for the actual diving with our myriad pieces of equipment. Also, bathroom facilities aboard will have to be modified from their present primitive state. The galley presents a problem in that it is now adequate for use by only its regular crew of 4 or 5—the captain, navigator, cook, and ordinary seamen. Since we will use a wireless operator besides ourselves, obviously the galley must be enlarged. At cursory glance, this had seemed a large boat; now in light of the number of persons needed aboard for the expedition, it appears we will be a bit crowded for space.

We decide to make our headquarters in Bethlehem at the Holy Land Christian Approach Mission while outfitting the ship and making other necessary preparations for the expedition.

"We're here", says Mike as gravel flies from beneath the car wheels on the inclined driveway in front of the Orphan Home. The gate man hurries down the steps to swing open the gates for us. We are at home again with our precious little orphan children who have stolen their way into our hearts. It is a heavy burden, but one I like, to have so many of them look upon me as their father.

Then I go over to our Mission's Crippled Children's Hospital to see our crippled children, "our dear bent-winged angels". My heart is ever touched —my eyes ever moist when I am at home with them, in a sense as their father as our beloved Mrs. Van der Linden is their mother. Mrs. Van, as we all know and love her, has for many years dedicated her life as nurse and supervisor to these crippled babies.

Next, I go to our Mission's Crippled Children's Convalescent Home, here to visit Miss Hilaneh Freij, who is the Matron of this division. Dear Hilaneh is known by all of the workers and children, in fact throughout Bethlehem, as the beloved Mother of our Mission.

Throughout the past years I have often been inspired and encouraged by Mrs. Van and Miss Hilaneh. When the road became rough and the burden almost too heavy, their dedicated services have always been inspirational to me.

During the six days we spend here while supervising the outfitting of the boats, the 100 workers and 300 orphans constantly swarm around every time they see me and pepper me with questions. The idea of diving into the Dead Sea is so foreign to them that they can't seem to believe their Director will actually try it. When I promise them they can watch me dive, excitement runs rampant. Every morning, before Dean and I make the drive down the winding Jericho road to the Dead Sea, they scamper toward us from all directions, asking if today they will watch us dive.

The day we arrive at the Mission, Dean and Naim take the single tank blocks to the Trade School, where an air compressor is installed, to let them be filling with air while we have our dinner. We want the tanks to be ready the first thing in the morning as we plan to take the boat out for a trial run and dive in the harbor area.

Early the next morning, a Friday, Dean, Mike, Naim and I return to the harbor, taking along Kheir Monsour, the supervisor of our Mission Trade School, and a local blacksmith. The latter two will take measurements and construct the necessary pieces according to our specifications.

We have overlooked the fact this is the Moslem Sabbath and run into difficulty at once. We ask to take the boat out a short distance to observe its operation, but there are no personnel available to operate it. Even a telephone call to the Colonel in charge of the headquarters in Amman gets no results. Finally, we have to be satisfied with doing only the measuring and calculating for the apparatus construction and return to Bethlehem without diving.

A few days later we do make our first dive for the purpose of testing weights, to see how many pounds will be needed to attain a neutral buoyancy.

Neutral buoyancy permits the diver to remain at any certain level underwater with the least possible exertion.

It is a well known fact that the more salt in the water, the more buoyancy will be experienced by anyone trying to swim or dive. Considering that the amount of salt in the ocean is about 5%, and in the Salt Lakes about 18%, the approximate 33% of solid matter, chiefly salt, in the Dead Sea makes the water so dense that a human body will float on the surface.

To solve the problem of submerging, we have brought along extra lead weights designed to slip onto our belts. For additional weight, I had intended buying lead here in Jordan. It was not available. Our search for lead ended at an Army rifle range in the Judean hills. Young boys gathered the spent lead bullets and brought us over 300 pounds of them. These were taken to the Trade School where the lead was melted and molded into blocks which could be strapped to our tanks. So, bullets from the new world linked with Bethlehem of the old world became the key to the door to the mysteries of the Dead Sea.

The responsibility of transferring all the gear and diving equipment to the naval craft has been given to Naim while Dean and I are busy talking to the captain. We are so thrilled at the prospect of our first dive into the Dead Sea that neither of us think to make an inventory of the gear. Fortunately, we have not planned to go out any great distance. Half a mile or so from the shore, the sailors drop anchor, and our tendermen begin assembling the equipment. Midway between zipping up the trouser legs of his suit and strapping on his tank block, Dean calls to Naim, "Bring me the weight belts and one of those heavier weights."

Naim throws his hands to his forehead in characteristic gesture.

"What's the matter with you? Come on, bring me the weights!" says Dean, getting warmer and more uncomfortable by the minute in his rubber suit.

"I can't, Mr. Dean. They're back on shore!" Naim wails.

Up comes the anchor, and we return to the dock. Naim is sent for the weights. He will not forget them next time.

Dean is to make the first experimental dive and wants to go down dressed in a full wet suit. I know he won't be able to submerge wearing a suit, even with considerable weight, but he insists so I agree. His jump from the high bow makes a tremendous splash into the 100 ft. deep water. But he comes to the surface quickly and floats on the surface. He fights the water, trying to force himself under, but all he does is lose a fin for his effort. Realizing he is fighting a losing battle, he swims to the boat.

He asks for more weight; we try varying amounts. Each dive results in frustration until, eventually, with one hundred more pounds of weights tied to his ankles, wrist, tank block, etc., Dean manages to get under the water. This experiment proves that we will not be able to wear these suits designed to keep divers warm during long or deep dives.

Dean, in his efforts to submerge, expends so much energy that he wisely decides not to follow the drop-line, which has been weighted with 100 lbs. of lead, any farther than about 30 feet. He breaks the surface and has a hard time unstrapping his weights and handing them to the sailors, high on the bow above him, without dropping them. Still carrying more than 150 lbs. of weights, he finds it almost impossible to climb up the ropes into the boat. We decide we cannot dive again until Mr. Monsour can build us a landing ramp on the boat.

Knowing now that the bow rides too high for us to dive off and get back with all the weights we will be carrying, I design a teeter-totter ramp,

hinged to the forward deck. When down, one end submerges about four feet under water. To get back aboard, one of us climbs onto this end, and six or seven sailors on the other end pull us up using their weight as leverage. Even so, after getting out of the water, they have to climb up and take off our weights before we can get down onto the deck. The weights are so heavy we cannot stand upright. The eighteen foot long ramp solves our problem neatly.

But, while the ramp is being constructed, I make another dive to determine the correct amount of weight needed to achieve the neutral buoyancy. Gearing up, I have Naim put thirty pounds of weights on my belt. This, together with Dean's belt which I also wear, gives me a total of sixty pounds. I figure this should be enough to take me under without wearing a wet suit.

I plummet into the water, then shoot to the surface. Adding more weights, I try again. Same result. And again, with added weights, no better luck. Finally, I start down with 150 pounds of weights tied to various parts of my anatomy and gear. I work my way down the shot line cautiously because even with all the weights, I still do not have proper ballast, and it would have taken too much strength to have tried to descend under my own power.

It is too late in the day to attempt a very deep dive. At 10 feet I stop to clear my ears, then go on, hand under hand. The water is about 60°, not too cold. I wonder when I will hit the thermic line, but never do. At about 20 feet I can no longer read my depth gauge as I have passed the twilight zone and am in completely dark water. It is an eerie feeling. The pressures seem to be greater in this extremely dense water, but I am reassured by the feel of the rope I am careful to grasp tightly. I decide at 50 feet this is far enough for the test of the weights and change course from down to up.

Ascending is easy. At 30 feet and again at 10 feet, I stop to decompress. Breaking the surface, I swim to the back of the boat and, after much struggling to untangle straps and weights, the sailors literally drag me on to the deck feeling like a fish out of water. Yes, by all means, the ramp which I have designed will be absolutely necessary for our return to the boat after every dive.

By now the sun has set. This is the Moslem Holy Season of Ramadan when no devout follower of Mohammed allows a morsel of food or water to pass his lips. Nor does he smoke between sunup and sundown. I know the captain and crew must be very hungry and thirsty, so I tell them to head for the dock while Dean and Naim help me ungear. Dean and I are also looking forward to getting fresh water ashore to wash off the oily Dead Sea waters and to get a cold drink of water. The oiliness of these waters is caused by the presence of chloride of calcium, and its extremely bitter taste by chloride of magnesium.

Testing of our weights on this trip proved fruitful in more ways than one. One startling discovery concerned the placing of the weights. We found that if they were not distributed properly, the part of the body overloaded tended to be pulled down, the rest following. To illustrate: on one of the testing dives, the weights at my belt had shifted so that I became top-heavy and suddenly found my head pulled down into the silt and mud. This problem of estimating the possible shift of weights underwater was a difficult one since we had no way of calculating this factor until going under. But we solved it by experimenting with weights on different parts of our bodies.

These experiences quickly convert us to deciding to dive only in swim trunks and perhaps a T-shirt to keep the many straps and belts from chafing the skin. Eventually, the total weight each of us will carry, including equipment and weights, comes to about 228 pounds. An 80 pound block of lead, molded from bullets, is attached to our double tank block and rigged for quick release should we have to surface in a hurry.

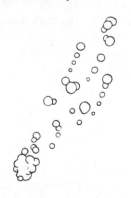

IX. WORLD'S BASEMENT

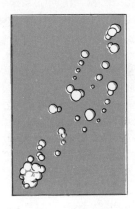

200 FEET BELOW—DEEPEST DIVE YET

Time was passing. With the test-diving at Akaba completed, the outfitting of the big boat for Sonar, coring and diving equipment finished, and the
proper weight distribution for Dead Sea diving established, Dean and I completed our plans for the
actual exploration of the fabulous Salt Sea. We must
get started very soon since the Jordan Valley is
characterized by very hot, dry, and long summers;
and by a relatively great number of very dry
khamsin (sirocco) days occurring mostly in the
spring. During these *khamsin* days a desert wind
blows from the east and brings with it fine desert

dust, causing the temperature to rise above 120°
F., and the humidity to rise sharply. These conditions we wanted to avoid, if at all possible; this
meant the expedition must get under way speedily.

Our plans called for intensive mapping and
charting of first the Khirbet Qumran area, with
exploratory dives if called for. Then to the Lisan
area for its Sonar charting and mapping. There
were good reasons for the order of operations. Dr.
Dejani, as well as Biblical scholars interested in
the Dead Sea Scrolls, had asked me to search carefully around Khirbet Qumran. Also, the geography
of the Dead Sea lent itself more readily to attack
in the Qumran area first.

Let me explain. The completely barren, Lisan
peninsula, jutting into the Dead Sea from the southeast, divides it into a larger and deeper northern
basin and a smaller and very shallow southern basin,
where the average depth is about 10 feet. The total
length of the Dead Sea from north to south is about
43 miles, and its width from east to west varies from
8 to 12 miles. The Dead Sea is really an inland lake
without outlet, its water level is maintained as a
result of the balance between the inflowing waters
of the Jordan River and a number of smaller
streams from the east and the loss due to evaporation. Since Qumran lay in the shallower northern
end, we decided to get our feet wet gradually, so
to speak, in that area. Also, we wanted to comply
with Dr. Dejani's request as soon as we could.

Before starting the actual operations, however, there were practical matters to be handled.

It had become quite a chore to make the drive from Bethlehem to the Dead Sea every morning while outfitting the boat and testing with weights. I decided to make our headquarters in the Dead Sea Hotel, on the seashore and adjacent to the area where the Dead Sea Scrolls had been found. We could save much-needed time by eliminating the drive. Also, even though I could not be staying at the Mission, I fully intended seeing that "my" orphans and crippled children had the chance to see my promised dive. The Dead Sea Hotel, I felt, provided the perfect location for the exhibition.

There was still another reason for my change of headquarters besides the convenience to the Qumran area. Although the expedition had, so far, progressed well, there were possible roadblocks still in its path to successful conclusion. Rumors had been reaching me that much skepticism was still evident in some of the higher circles of government. Certain people were expressing the opinion that it was impossible to dive beneath the waters of the Dead Sea. And this attitude was quite natural. For, due to the unusual weight of this water, with its high concentration of chemicals, even people unable to swim can easily float on it. I could appreciate their doubt, but I felt the disbelief in the possibility of diving beneath these waters and staying down had to be dispelled in a dramatic fashion, or we could be delayed at a crucial moment and find ourselves unable to continue because of the sirocco.

Being from Missouri, where the slogan is "Show Me", I, naturally, considered the idea of

making an actual dive in the presence of as many high-placed officials as I could invite. With the Dead Sea Hotel in such an advantageous spot for an exhibition dive, I could "kill several birds" with one stone, so to speak. Our beloved orphans and crippled children would get their promise fulfilled; the skeptics would observe an actual dive and know the truth; and, I could, at the same time, complete my final testing before the actual work of the expedition began. For, I intended making this a very deep dive—a first of its kind in the Dead Sea.

The very next morning, I called Mike Handel into my office at the Mission, informed him of my plan, and asked him to arrange a picnic in front of the Dead Sea Hotel within the next few days. I told him our expedition party would be moving to the Hotel that day, and as soon as I could invite several dignitaries, I would notify him, and he could then transport the children there. He suggested that since my birthday had occurred while I was diving at Akaba, and the children had been unable to celebrate the occasion, perhaps they could make the picnic a birthday party for their 'father', meaning me. I was touched and agreed, of course.

The expedition party traveled down to the Dead Sea Hotel the next day, Thursday, and were given simple accommodations. I contacted several members of Parliament, the Mayor of Bethlehem, and the governor of the district to invite them to the demonstration dive. This was set for Monday. The purpose of the dive, as far as the dignitaries were concerned, was to provide entertainment for the children at the picnic. I, of course, had other reasons.

The breezes coming off the sea were zephyr-like; the sea itself, calm; the day promised perfection. I was ready for the proceedings; the guests will come this afternoon but the Mission children are due to arrive any moment. Ah, here they come in four large busses rolling to a stop in formation. The teachers are helping the little ones out while the drivers unload one of the busses which is carrying the band uniforms, instruments, picnic supplies, and food. I go to greet them and am engulfed in a wave of youngsters, clapping their hands and shouting, "Happy Birthday, Dear Dr. Baney!" Through a lump in my throat, I tell the children to "take it easy." Then, hugging as many of them as I can reach, I tell Mrs. Van der Linden, supervisor, to lead them to the picnic area adjacent to the hotel.

At that, the happy mob breaks loose from me, and the children troop straight for the wet sand to get into the water if they can. Soon, trousers are wet to the top, dresses droop and dangle with sea water, and a regular line of forts, houses, and sea-castles begins to spring up along the beach.

When lunch time comes, all the workers help the little ones enjoy a beach dinner of eggs, potatoes, green onions, bread, and Jericho bananas for dessert. Then, off come braces and shoes and stockings, and small atrophied legs feel the tickling of the salt water surf. Some of the disabled plunge directly into the surf, out of the reach of their guardians.

Our children from Bethlehem arrive in buses for my long promised picnic, fun on the beach, swimming and diving demonstration.

Nurses aid our "bent-winged angels" from the buses to the sandy beach.

I rush to the shore, cautioning the nurses to keep a sharp lookout; the lives of these children have been given into our keeping in trust, and they must be cherished and guarded at all times.

The frolicking is not marred by any accident, and "my" youngsters have a wonderful time splashing and floating. Dean informs me that the invited guests are arriving and, it's just as well, as some of the children are beginning to ask about the demonstration I had promised them.

Inside the hotel, I put on my yellow diving suit. When I come out, the children are gleeful at my novel appearance. The nurses and teachers herd them down toward the pier where the guests will observe my dive from the Jordanian Naval Craft furnished by His Majesty, King Hussein. This is the boat we have spent the last week outfitting.

When order among the children is restored, and they are lined up to watch, I walk into the surf and make a special short dive just for them. They are beside themselves when I surface.

Afterwards, the distinguished guests pass by the tables of equipment on the beach, and I explain all these items used in diving. I tell my guests this will be the first deep dive ever made into the Dead Sea. They listen politely, but here and there among them, I detect incredulous looks. To impress on them that this is no job for a thrill-seeker or amateur, so they will understand my dedication to this mission, I inform them that it would be easy to strangle if one were to swallow this water because of a faulty mask or too little

Orphan Home Band provides a concert for the occasion.

training. The seriousness of this dive begins to penetrate; several of them pay closer attention.

Just then a man, carrying sound-recording equipment, approaches and tells me he is a broadcaster from Jerusalem. He asks permission to tape my demonstration dive. He says the tape will be re-broadcast at the Jerusalem radio station. I can see this will help the expedition and agree on the condition that he lets me hear the tape first, for editing. The broadcaster will go aboard, observe the dive, and report it on tape.

It occurs to me that it will be quite interesting to compare my underwater observations with those topside, and I tell him I will be honored to have him broadcast the proceedings on his 'weekly spot interviews with interesting people,' as he calls it.

The photographer is busily taking pictures of the assemblage as the Jerusalem broadcaster, Dean, and I leave the pier in the Naval craft. I tell the captain to take us out to where the sea is about 200 feet deep. This will not be too far out, and the spectators will be able to observe practically everything that takes place on the dive.

I explain to the broadcaster and the notables aboard that, making allowances for the drift of the boat, this dive would be to a depth of 170 to 200 feet. As I am explaining, the broadcaster sets up his recorder and the captain anchors the boat.

In order to establish beyond any doubt that I would dive down to the dark bottom of the Dead Sea, I had hit upon the idea of lowering a

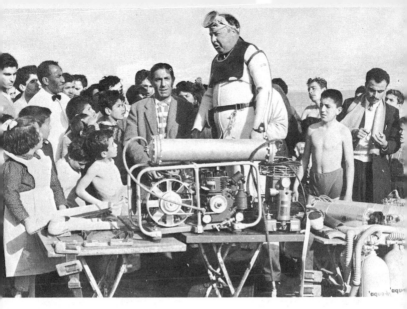

Dean and I introduce SCUBA diving to our inquisitive children and guests.

rope-line, with knots every 25 feet in it and a 100 pound weight tied to the end, over the side of the boat to the bottom. So that everyone aboard should see this was a valid test, I asked the sailors to measure out 200 feet of rope, tie the knots at 25 feet intervals, and then attach the 100 pound weight at the 200 foot point. With this done, I then offer to bring up some concrete and visible proof from the bottom to show I had actually been there.

Dean now helps me gear up. He placed the lead weights—approximately 200 pounds—in the proper places. I crawl onto the landing ramp, ready to dive into the water. Turning, I wave to Dean, bow my head in prayer for a moment, then go into the water with a deep splash. I go under at once, grabbing the rope-line.

I pull myself down hand under hand feeling for the first knot. I am able to check my depth gauge for only the first few feet. As I slowly descend to the 10 foot mark, the twilight zone closes in and becomes deep night. From here on I am in completely dark water, and the temperature becomes noticeably cooler.

Cautiously, I begin popping my ears, each time I reach another knot. These knots seem to be stretched farther and farther apart now. Funny, I had been sure they were exactly 25 ft. apart! Perhaps it is only imagination . . . the distance between them . . . Oh, well . . .

I notice I am experiencing a small amount of mask-squeeze; I adjust and pause. Where is that next knot? I slide my hand slowly and then more

For orphan children and guests—a demonstration of the expedition's diving equipment and techniques.

quickly downward. Ah, there it is. The blackness is getting to me.

Having kept count of the knots, I know where I am, but the time seems interminable before I will hit bottom. Every so often I give a series of jerks on the line to reassure both Dean and myself that I'm all right and still kicking. My breathing apparatus and equipment are working perfectly, and I have no difficulty such as I had had in the Red Sea.

But, where, oh where is the bottom? My faith in the Sonar remains strong but the darkness makes me very uneasy. The knots tell me the 100 pound weight must be close, but the last one must be at least a half-mile farther down. Or so it seems. Suddenly, my fin jars a surface. I'm down at the bottom of the Dead Sea!

Utter darkness walls me in as though I were in a crypt. I begin feeling around warily, hoping to find some extraordinary object to carry back with me. Instead, I grab nothing but silt. Running my left arm down almost to the shoulder, my hand snubs against a hard surface. Scratching around for a solid substance — a stone or maybe a tree-branch — I find nothing. Realizing my scant remaining air supply will not allow me to remain any longer, allowing for stops at various levels to decompress, I grab a very big handful of this black mud in my left hand, and with relief, reach for the first knot upward with my right. How close it seems! And the next and the next!

It is awkward, scrambling upward with one hand since I don't dare release the mud from my

left hand. My motion resembles a land crab sidling with a crippled claw.

Finding the 100 foot mark, I pause for a few moments. Then, at the 50 foot mark, I stop again for about three minutes, carefully clutching my evidence and holding tightly to the ladder to the open sky. I ascend from this point, almost too quickly, exhaling heavily all the while, until I am at 10 feet below the surface. The visibility lightens, thank God, and I rest here to decompress for about four minutes, a safe margin.

Seconds later, mud in hand, I break the surface to the accompaniment of a great shout from the boat and the shore. The band starts playing, the children jump up and down shouting and waving, and the crowd claps their hands appreciatively. I glance at my watch. I have been under almost an hour!

The broadcaster has a stunned, almost incredulous look on his face. I wonder how he is describing my dive as he talks into his microphone. Right now, I am anxious to get to shore and hear the reaction of the notables and to see my orphans again before time for them to return to Bethlehem.

Once on shore, the ecstatic glances and the excited maulings of my children are proof enough of their affection and provide the finest birthday present I'd ever had.

The afternoon is coming to a close. At 5:00 P.M. the buses load up; the children call, "Shukrin (thank you) Dr. Baney," and the journey back to

Dean and tendermen gear me up for demonstration dive.

Bethlehem begins. I wave goodbye until they are out of sight.

Dean and I invite our guests into the hotel for refreshments amidst a general hubbub, and he made them comfortable until I could get dressed and join the gathering. By this time, the broadcaster from Jerusalem had been circulating among them, and it is evident he has helped convince them of the authenticity of the dive.

In a short while, after many congratulatory expressions, most of the guests left. Dean and I made our excuses and escaped to our rooms to discuss the events of the day. I was happy and exhilarated for obviously the demonstration had been a success, and I had convinced many people, once and for all, that a dive could be made to the bottom of the Dead Sea.

Later that evening, I played back the tape left by the broadcaster. Here, in essence, are his words:

"Ladies and Gentlemen, this is Jerusalem Broadcasting. This is our weekly spot interview with interesting people who make the news. This week we are not in Jerusalem but at the Dead Sea for the purpose of having an interview with Dr. Ralph Baney and the members of his Baney Dead Sea Expedition. We are aboard the Jordanian Naval Craft which His Majesty, King Hussein has placed at Dr. Baney's disposal for the duration of this Dead Sea Expedition.

"This afternoon Dr. Baney will make his first extensive test dive deep into the Dead Sea. For

this occasion, we understand Dr. Baney has invited other archaeologists, notables, and representatives of His Majesty's services to witness this event.

"As we pull away from shore, Dr. Baney has given the order for the ship to be taken to where the water is 170 to 200 feet deep. While the ship advances to this point, Dr. Baney explains that the Sonar equipment aboard has charted the exact spot.

"The ship is anchored and a long line with knots in it and a 100 pound weight on the end of it is dropped overboard here. This line is 200 feet long.

"Mr. Ryther assists Dr. Baney by placing approximately 200 pounds of weights on his back and around his body. This will keep him under and take him to the bottom, we are told. I request Dr. Baney to bring back a stone, or silt, or mud to prove he has actually been on the bottom.

"On the landing platform, built out from the bow of the boat, Dr. Baney puts in his mouthpiece. He is bowing his head in prayer. He turns his head, waves, and plunges in. There is a tremendous splash. We see his air bubbles as he begins to sink. He disappears, and all we can see are smaller and smaller air bubbles as he goes deeper . . .

"It is now 4:45 P.M., and according to our time, Dr. Baney has been under the water some 20 minutes. Bubbles on the surface are the only sign of his presence. Mr. Ryther has a serious expression on his face and I ask him if everything is all right. He assures me that Dr. Baney is a skilled diver and in any other sea or ocean he would have no fear, but in this strange sea and carrying so many weights, a depth of 200 feet would be comparable to 230 feet or more in any other water because of the difference in pressures . . . There is nothing to do for the moment but wait.

"Ladies and gentlemen, on checking my watch, I find that almost an hour has elapsed since Dr. Baney went beneath these waters. The air aboard ship is becoming charged with tension as we all realize that this is the first real dive that has ever been made into this Sea.

"Everyone is very still, and we watch Mr. Ryther as he signals periodically to Dr. Baney by a series of jerks on the drop-line which extends to the bottom. Dr. Baney is holding on to this line as he descends and can also communicate with his master diver.

"Just a moment . . . I believe we have a response from Dr. Baney! Yes, there is! He is signalling he is "okay".

"We are all sighing in relief. We presume he will soon be coming up. The air has become quite chilly. The sun will soon be going down, and it is increasingly difficult for us to see the bubbles on the surface of the water.

"The bubbles are becoming larger, and Mr. Ryther tells us this means the diver is ascending. The bubbles are about the size of an orange, and each time he rises several more feet, they grow bigger. I understand that since Dr. Baney is in total darkness below 25 feet, both his ascent and descent must be gauged by measuring the knots on the diving line. I am told when a diver is returning to the

surface after a deep dive, he must stop at certain levels and remain there for so many minutes to decompress and allow the nitrogen in his blood to dissipate.

"Mr. Ryther now has a happier expression on his face as he has been jerking on the drop-line and has received an answer. He tells me Dr. Baney is fine and wants a brass band waiting, a 2-pound Kansas City steak, and a gallon of hot coffee when he comes up!

"The bubbles are getting larger. This means he is nearing the surface. Mr. Ryther says that Dr. Baney is still in completely dark water and will have to come up another 50-100 feet to pause for decompression. The last time he will stop will be about 25 feet below the surface, and this will be the final stage of decompression.

"The bubbles are the size of footballs now and there is restlessness in the watchers here on board. Several have been skeptical that he could reach the bottom, and of course, everyone is frankly amazed at the duration of this dive. Although we hope he will bring us visible evidence from the bottom, still we will be glad to see him surface . . . this has been a long wait.

"Ladies and gentlemen, the bubbles are increasing to the size of an inner tube! This is an exciting moment, and a spontaneous cheer goes up as he is emerging from the water . . . We can see he is holding something in his left hand. Here he comes onto the landing platform and is handing Mr. Ryther a fistful of . . . it's mud! Mud from the bottom of the Dead Sea! Wonderful! Wonderful!

"Ladies and gentlemen . . . Here is dramatic proof that by skill and daring, this diver, Dr. Baney, has actually gone down 200 feet to the very bottom of the Dead Sea!"

That was the end of the tape. When I realized that this broadcast would reach practically everyone in Jordan, I felt wonderful. I couldn't have done better if I'd arranged it.

Now, with the doubters convinced, my test dives all completed, we were ready for the work of charting and mapping the most promising areas of this Sea of Lot. Tomorrow we will start.

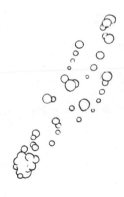

X SHORELINE SURVEY

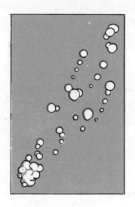

ABOVE AND BELOW

Before actually starting on the many Sonar charting runs, I felt a general shoreline survey of the entire Dead Sea might give us a historical perspective in keeping with the scientific aspects of the Expedition. Accordingly, I informed the captain to get the craft ready for a trip starting early in the morning. Then I inspected the Sonar equipment carefully. For the first time, the shoreline will be 'seen' from both above and below the water.

Daybreak found us aboard and looking forward to the excursion with feelings of anticipation.

A mist, hung upon jade, blue-shadowed waters, made the mountains on the eastern side look like a cloud of lavender suspended in the sky. The heat came in waves. Before us lay the Dead Sea and the dead world that lies about it.

To the south I see the green of the water merge into a leprous white that might have been a scar on the earth's surface. On closer view the more vivid white takes the shape of salt-pans; the rest is a desert of naked marl hills, flat-topped, fantastic in shape, and pale as death.

We cast off, following closely the northwestern bank. The Sonar begins its clicking and drawing; the picture unfolds. A vulture wheels above us, a big white bird with black on its wings. This is the Egyptian vulture. It will bathe in only a few inches of water and then sit on a rock to dry. The lines of the Sonar peak evenly across the chart. The water spread before me is a sparkling blue. We begin the survey from the Naval base around the northern end. The Sonar picks up some interesting data as we pass between the Dead Sea Hotel and the little island standing alone in the front of it. This will certainly be worthy of exploration later. Next, the mouth of the Jordan yawns in our wake with its big mud flats surrounding it. The Jordan delta merges into a plain then narrows to a point about five miles southward down the east bank. At this point the eastern shoreline looks like a solid wall at the water's edge. For twenty-five miles, cliffs of Nubian sandstone rise up from the depths of the sea, leaving no room for a beach

Cliffs of vari-colored Nubian sandstone wall in the waters of the Dead Sea.

or a road on the shore. There are a few little breaks where small streams come down in the rainy season through narrow gorges from the plateau to the sea but none of them is passable; not even the Arnon, the largest, because of numerous rapids and waterfalls. Beyond those cliffs is the mountainous land of Moab from which Ruth and Naomi emigrated to Bethlehem.

In this sea, I reflect, no living creature could survive. Nor does it seem strange that this should be so. For, despite the color and sunlight, the atmosphere is sinister and oppressive, as of a place accursed. Scientific data supports the fact also; statistics prove its deadliness. No fish, no seaweed, no coral grow here, and no vegetation upon its banks. This remarkable body of water, 43 miles long by ten to twelve miles wide, lies 1,274 feet below the level of the Mediterranean, and in the northern part, is more than 1,300 feet deep. Shut in between steep and barren hills on either side, it is not only the lowest point on the earth's surface — the world's basement — but also the most salty body of water in the world, for it contains some 33% of solid matter, including common salt, bromide, magnesium chloride, and calcium chloride. Its excessive density is the result entirely of evaporation, for the streams which empty their waters into the Dead Sea contain no more solid matter than is normal. However, the heat is so tremendous that the loss of water more than keeps pace with the intake. The water is singularly unpleasant to the taste, being like a concentrated dose of Epsom salts. It is also ex-

tremely painful if it gets into the eyes or any cut or sore.

We journey on, on past the towering Nubian cliffs. Here stands Macaerus, the formidable stronghold built by Herod the Great, where John the Baptist was imprisoned and beheaded by the younger Herod. This fortress was built on a very high rock with deep ravines on every side, and enclosed by a great wall that had hundred-foot towers at the corners. Near it were many springs, some bitter and some sweet, of a variety of temperatures, including two that flowed from two rocks like fountains, one hot and the other cold.

Here, the Dead Sea is a dull pale blue, and the hills that wall it in are of yellows and purples and blues and browns so dull that such words for color are almost too vivid to refer to them. One of these hills is Mt. Nebo, from which Moses looked across to the Promised Land.

Past the Wadi Mujeb where the Arnon flows into the Sea, now, after some distance the cliffs begin to recede and leave quite a long narrow beach-like plain for the last ten miles of the coast. Sonar peaks begin to appear on the charts. This dry, rocky and gravel plain gradually blends into a fertile oasis surrounding the Lisan Cove area. From the northern part of this section, the Lisan peninsula extends to within two miles of the east bank. The 'Tongue', itself, extends six miles into the sea from the east leaving only a narrow strait between it and Masada on the west shore. Here is the shallowest part of the sea, and in Roman times

In several areas we found both hot and cold, fresh water springs at the shoreline and on the sea floor.

it was shallower still, so that it was actually forded at times. The 'tongue' and shallow narrows divide the sea into two quite different parts. To the north, the sea bottom drops down sharply from a few feet to as much as 1,310 feet below the surface while the southern end is really just a large shallow bay, for the most part from five to ten feet deep. Chugging along, I am impressed by the different appearance and color of the deep, original northern part and the shallow southern bay merging into a barren waste of glistening salt marsh and desolate mud. Looking toward the shoreline, it is difficult to tell just where the sea ends and the marsh begins.

We skirt the peninsula and journey slowly onward. My mind is filled with images of olden times and the drama which had played itself out in antiquity. Rounding the extreme southern curve of the Dead Sea, I observed it passing almost imperceptibly into the barren waste of the Sebkha, the glistening salt marsh in which the wadis lose themselves, a flat plain of soft, impassable mud. The Sonar picture contrasts oddly with my visual perception.

The surface of the Dead Sea is usually calm and, because of its great density, is not easily ruffled by a light breeze. However, the strong winds which pour down the western slopes in late afternoon can stir up very choppy water and during the rainy season quite dangerous storms may develop. Rain is rare, the average for the year being only two inches, but when it does fall, it is likely to come as a very heavy thunderstorm.

It is just such an eventuality I wish to avoid, so I tell the captain to speed up the trip. The Sonar clicks merrily along.

As I look northward along the west shore, I see it is quite different from the rock wall close to the east side. There are steep and jagged rocky cliffs, but they are not so high. Between them and the water there is room for a gravel beach and a pathway which is still used by the Bedouins for limited local travel by donkey back.

This area on the western shore of the Dead Sea is the dry and barren wilderness of Judea, devoid of vegetation except for a faint shadow of grass which appears on the north side of the hills for a brief time in the spring. In pleasant contrast there are four important springs at intervals along the shore which produce little oases of green down near the water's edge. One of these, Ain Feshka, is not far from the ruins of the Qumran monastery where the Dead Sea Scrolls were found.

As we travel slowly northward, hugging the western bank of the Dead Sea, the excursion is nearing its end, the Sonar is completing its picture —the first that has ever been made beneath the waters of the Dead Sea shore line, portraying a pictorial view of the shoreline bed of this sea. We have almost completely encircled this Sea of Death, and only a small part remains to be observed until we anchor at the Naval Base.

The landscape of the Dead Sea wilderness is monotonous, subduing, and dreadful. It is a landscape without features: no faces of earthly gods

The bleak wilderness of Judea as it converges upon the western shores of the Dead Sea.

or men, no bodies of recumbent animals are suggested by the shapes of the hills. The already
fading grass of spring has the look of greenish
mold on enormous loaves. Tawny without warmth,
of a dun not enriched by shadows, the hills also
somewhat resembled the humps of the camels that
grazed, dull yellow and gawkily bending, with the
dusty white calves beside them. One hillside is

flecked by a herd of black goats. Here and there, all alone in the emptiness, squats motionless a Bedouin woman keeping an eye on a camel or goat.

We are steaming nearer now to the ruins of the Qumran monastery and our journey is coming to an end. Along the shoreline, the all but bare ground is rusted with streaks of some reddish plant, and dabbed here and there with statice, a dreary little white herb. The only forms of vertebrate life I see are a hawk and a crow contending for some small animal that the crow has caught but that the hawk has forced him to drop. The crow is reluctant to leave its prey, but the hawk keeps circling, incisively and slowly, and the crow keeps a sharp watch on him. There are scorpions and vipers here. The scene recalls that "great and terrible wilderness" of which Moses speaks in Deuteronomy 8:15, with its "fiery serpents and scorpions and thirsty ground, where there is no water."

Scanning this landscape, one is aware of neither light nor darkness. It is as if one were sunk below them; to live here seems a kind of self-burial.

Yet it is here I have followed my vision, in a sincere effort to unlock and penetrate these waters to reveal historic and Biblical truths of God's Hand in His destruction by fire and brimstone of these wicked cities of Sodom and Gomorrah. The awful desolation of the area is a reminder of the fate of those cities of ill-repute, destroyed by the wrath of God as a lesson to mankind saving only Lot, a good man, and his two daughters. This

A four foot long desert lizard which I outran and captured near the Dead Sea. These ugly creatures are greatly feared by local inhabitants.

expedition will, I believe, uncover some evidence of their devastation.

And now, where our craft is slowly passing, the Essenes once resorted to worship God and to save their souls from infamies; to turn away from the Way of Darkness and follow the Way of Light.

The ruins of their monastery still stands, as was noted by Pliny, some distance away from the shore. I gaze in solemn contemplation at its gray blocks of stone. The cliff rises steeply behind it and I note, here and there, the dark cracks of natural caves such as the ones in which the Scrolls were found. The Sonar reveals that the terrain above is merging gradually into the water making a sloping incline.

The evening shadows are gathering, and the trip is nearly completed. We pass the ruins of the monastery with its cemetery of a thousand graves and continue around the curve of the Sea until the Naval Base comes into view.

We anchor; the excursion is done. My feelings cannot be put into words; I have been a worshipful spectator at the unfolded drama of the Bible in this part of the theater in which it was played. My faith and determination are revitalized and reinforced;—this expedition will be, I believe, a fulfillment of my vision.

XI PURSUIT

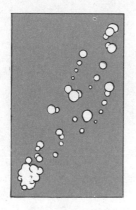

IN WATERS LAPPING AT THE CAVES
OF THE DEAD SEA SCROLLS

Qumran, Khirbet Qumran—A locale, now world-famous as the repository for the Dead Sea Scrolls. The brooding bluffs pocked with the cavern openings . . . the imagination-stirring terraces of broken cliffs, plateaus, rubble . . . stories of ancient times scribbled indelibly on the high levels down to the shoreline . . . and perhaps on in . . . into the sea itself.

Here, in this place, secreting Biblical truths, is the area Dr. Dejani and eminent Biblical scholars suggest the first operations of the expedition begin.

I am happy to oblige. I, too, feel the urge to roll back the covers of history from the book of man's life and bring to light verification of God's Word. There can be no better starting point.

We do not literally plunge right in. No, very carefully, Dean and I review each step of our planning. The operations will take place in four well-defined and separate moves: first, the mapping and charting of the entire area of the sea bed from the shoreline out to about three miles with the Sonar. Next in order, after analyzing the charts, a recharting of the most promising areas. The follow-up step: running back over the likeliest points to drop marker buoys. And finally, the diving along the marker buoy track to bring up, if we can, material evidence of what the Sonar has located.

In the telling, the operations seem fairly cut and dried. In the doing, however, we are quite aware that this kind of work has never before been attempted. No one else has paved our way in the Dead Sea; we have no guideposts or blueprints to follow. We will be blazing a new pathway in the uncharted wastelands of oceanography. Not until we perform these operations will we know the hazards and perils to be faced, fought, and conquered and find the evidence to support my theories.

The evening before we start operations, Dean and I pore over the working map. Pointing to several areas, starting from a point about two miles down the coast from where we are now situated at the Dead Sea Hotel, I tell Dean:

"Here, here, and here should be the starting

locations. I have an idea the general topography below water should be pretty much the same as that above."

Since we are on the veranda and the evening is bright with moonlight, Dean can see the area to which I am referring. High up, overlooking the dashing waves there, the cliffs loom menacingly, partly in shadow, their weird shapes sprawl in jagged poses down to a flat, level plateau; then the walls take up an unbroken march downward to the ground. From their base to the water's edge a gentle slope inclines, disappearing gradually into the dark blue of the sea. There is little or no vegetation, the crops here are stones and boulders. The face of the cliffs look wrinkled, the folds hide cave openings. It is here, in one of these miniature caverns, that the history-making Dead Sea Scrolls had been discovered.

"I'm right with you, Doc. The landscape over there surely looks inviting for our first runs. What do you say we close up shop for now and get an early start in the morning?"

I fold the map, nodding in agreement. Tomorrow, and other tomorrows will unreel, I hope, the story of those long-departed days. May it please God for me to have a small part in this unfolding drama. I go to bed, and fall asleep with this prayer in my heart.

Up very early the following morning we eat breakfast, eager to get to the dock. The morning mists shroud the craft in ghostly outlines but soon the sun drives them away. We go aboard and care-

fully check the equipment to see that everything is ready; and, at long last, the engines cough into a steady roar. The captain orders the anchor lifted and we are on our way to the Great Adventure.

The sea is calm, an auspicious omen for the beginning. We start our first run after taking bearings on three landmarks so as to get a fix for the compass. The fix will give us our exact location in relation to the shore, saving us from repeating the charting over the same areas at another time. The Sonar sounding away hollowly is making the zig-zag lines on the chart.

The first run goes along the shoreline from the area of Khirbet Qumran, out about 300 feet. We cannot keep a straight course since the depth close in to shore varies. We continue practically parallel to this west bank of the Dead Sea for a distance of about eighteen miles, running the Sonar all the way. The direction of the run is southward. Qumran lies in the northwestern sector of the Dead Sea. Our third point of bearing — a huge boulder extending into the sea — limits our run. Here we turn and make the return run exactly parallel to the first one, all the way back to our starting point. The runs are about 100 feet apart. At the original point, we turn again and make another run parallel to the second until we again reach the boulder landmark. All our runs are made in this pattern until we have covered an area approximately three miles out from the shoreline. Here the depth becomes greater than 300 feet — the limits of our Sonar. In this way, the entire Qumran area is charted by Sonar. From an overhead view, the runs would present a series of furrows similar to those plowed in a huge field by a farmer.

All these runs and the resulting Sonar marking on the charts did not take place all in the same day. If we were fortunate we could stay out several hours at a time. Many days storms prevented our sailing, engines broke down, one of us became ill or suffered from too much sun, for innumerable reasons the crew could not work. Unforeseen events were continually hampering our plans, so we were happy if, at the end of a day, we had new charts to examine and analyze preparatory to mapping out the next day's run. Originally I had thought the Qumran area could be covered in five to six days; almost two weeks were to go by before we could extend operations to the southern or Lisan area.

After the first few runs, we are champing at the bit, so to speak. The peaks and valleys are beginning to show up on the Sonar charts in interesting fashion, and Dean wants to go underwater every time a 'blip' marks an unusual peak. I remind him of our plans; we want to completely cover the area before starting the follow up steps. Inwardly though, I agree with him. It is becoming harder to restrain the impulse to go down immediately and see if I can find anything tangible.

The original runs over the Qumran area are finished in four days. Then, Dean and I work out the reruns over the areas which look most promising. The Sonar charts indicate unusual peaks at the lower end of our runs; we head for this area and

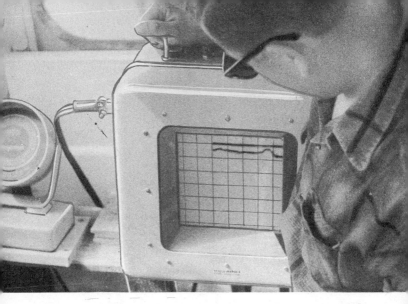

begin recharting. Two more days and we are ready
to retrace the verified spots for our marker buoy
dropping.

These shining, yellow buoys will pinpoint exact
locations for our exploratory dives. We do not drop
them indiscriminately; only the most promising
markings of the Sonar charts receive these spotters.

By now our runs have covered every foot of
this Qumran area, and the reruns have verified some
highly unusual configurations on the sea floor, especially in the immediate vicinity of the Dead Sea
Scroll caves. We make the marker buoy run, setting a line of them, and prepare for exploratory
dives.

We drop the first of the buoys close to our
starting point. Here the charts have indicated 'tells'
or mounds, or something worthwhile investigating.

Continuing, buoys are set in a line extending all the way to the extreme end of our boundaries to the south, beyond the Ain Feshka section of the Qumran area. All in all, nine 'tells,' according to the charts, seem to be hiding below. These hillocks, jutting upward from the sea floor, are within one-half mile of the shoreline; most of them are just opposite to where the Dead Sea Scrolls were found. Of course, all of them differ in size, from a typical burial tomb, to the size of a fortress or small ancient city. This fact convinces me that this had been an inhabited plain, used for farming until it was inundated at some period in history by the Dead Sea.

The pattern assuming shape on the charts begins to show that the plain sloping from the caves about one-half mile to the shoreline extends under the water for about one and one-half miles to where the incline drops off abruptly and becomes a very steep bluff. The Sonar cannot chart below the bluff as, apparently, the depth is beyond 300 feet to the sea bottom here. There is a gradual descent of around fifty feet from the shoreline to the drop-off. This Sonar pattern seems to verify my theory. And I am becoming quite anxious to go down and see for myself.

We finish setting the marker buoys; exploratory dives will be our next operation.

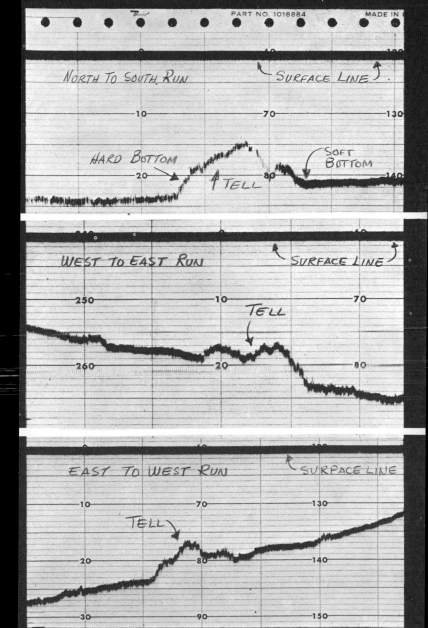

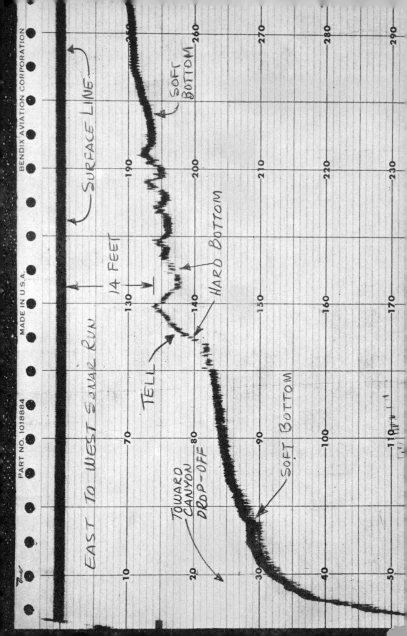

EAST TO WEST SONAR RUN

SURFACE LINE

TOWARD CANYON DROP-OFF

TELL

14 FEET

HARD BOTTOM

SOFT BOTTOM

SOFT BOTTOM

BENDIX AVIATION CORPORATION

MADE IN U.S.A.

PART NO. 1018884

XII CITADEL

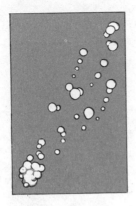

INVASION OF HER HIDDEN CHAMBERS

There is an outpost of the Jordanian Army in the vicinity of the Khirbet Qumran area. Because the country hereabout is virtually uninhabited, the targets on their firing range are situated so that soldiers shooting from the hills spatter gunshot into the sea. It so happens that some of the most promising 'tells' and mounds are located in this same area. Before planning a day's run in the boat for Sonar charting, or for diving offshore from Qumran, it is necessary to check with the officer of the day at the Army post to find out if target practice

is scheduled. Quite often there is no need to call him since the sound of gunfire at daybreak is notice enough.

Eight or ten of our floats marking the location of 'tells' have been in the water for about five days. Friday, out of respect for the Moslem Sabbath, we could not take the boat away from the dock. On Saturday there was a storm. Sunday we were at the Mission in Bethlehem for services and conferences. On Monday, again it rained wildly. We knew we were pushing our luck leaving the floats in the water for so many days without retrieving them, but we had no choice.

We get up before sunrise. Tuesday morning dawns bright and clear. Jabra packs lunches, and we prepare to spend the entire day diving — exploring the sea floor marked by our floats. But before we can reach the harbor, the loud noise of artillery fire splits the air and echoes among the hills.

"Holy cow!" says Dean, "There go the floats!"

This is not the first time our floats have disappeared from the water. Evidently the soldiers cannot resist the shining yellow buoys floating on the Dead Sea. So, we waste no time at the harbor. The boat captain telephones army headquarters to ask that the firing be halted so we can board the boat and begin the day's diving schedule. The conversation becomes heated. Finally the captain hangs up and tells me the best he can do is to get the soldiers to stop firing at 10:00 o'clock.

The firing ceases, and we move out of the harbor toward where our floats are supposed to be.

They are gone — all except one sad little pouch holding a bubble of air. One side of it is riddled with holes. This is the last of our yellow plastic floats. They were expensive, and we had brought only thirty of them, thinking that would be enough. From this time on, we collect bottles which the boys paint red. Corked and anchored they do the job as well as floats and serve us well everywhere except in the Qumran area where the soldiers repeatedly pick them off like clay pigeons. Disconcerting as this is, we have to give the soldiers credit for being good marksmen.

Even though our charts are already marked, today we will make reruns in order to pinpoint again where we are to dive. The day is perfect for diving, and we have come prepared. Dean will make the first dive at the spot marked by the remaining float. If his findings confirm our expectations, we will continue diving here the rest of the day. To make sure we are in the right spot, we turn on the Sonar equipment and make several runs across the 'tell' which is sixteen feet below the surface.

We are without tendermen this morning as Mike and Naim are in Bethlehem. One of us has to stay on board, so I help Dean gear up and watch as he plunges in. In this dive Dean is in the water forty-five minutes and covers an area about 100 feet in diameter.

This dive, as well as the others we make in the ensuing days, is indeed exploratory in more ways

than one. Described coldly and unemotionally these
immersions might give the impression of being easy,
everyday events of no great difficulty. The contrary is true, however. Each time one of us goes
under in this foul, chemical-laden syrupy Sea, the
conditions are extremely strenuous. No one who
has not experienced it, can quite get the sensation.
Every foot downward is a trip into what seems a
bottomless, suffocating pit slowly closing in on you.
With all the weights on our backs, belts, ankles, and
waists pulling us down, it's like squeezing into a
pitch black cubby-hole, narrowing to a point at the
bottom, until one is caught in a void where movements are sluggish, the pressure of the water op-
pressing, breathing becomes tortured, muscles tight-
en, lips swell from exertion, and lungs burn as if

from desert air. One has ventured into a world within a world, pioneering not only physical trails but also emotional pathways into surrealistically different feelings, impressions, sensations, and observations.

So, to say that Dean and I make dives of only 45 minutes duration and cover areas 100 feet in diameter, can only give a skeleton account of such a dive and its attendant difficulties. But, with all the newness and harshness of these experiences, we are constantly spurred on by our discoveries and continue with unabated desire.

The Sonar has given us the spots to search; in our explorations around Khirbet Qumran we locate, literally by hand alone, nine 'tells,' in staggered formation. In our first dives we also come across numerous small trees partially covered by silt with their roots still in mud. These trees are not brittle or rotten; rather, they seem almost petrified by the concentrated chemicals of the water.

So far as the 'tells' are concerned, we find great variance in the silt. Its depth ranges from approximately six inches to three feet. I consider the evidence gathered from the preliminary exploratory dives worthy of continued activity in at least five of the nine 'tells.'

The 'tells' are composed of heaps of stones. The most promising and largest of them is located practically on the bank of the Wadi Qumran. The others lie all around it in scattered formation. Feeling the ground around them, we find the sea bottom here to be rather smooth with a crust perhaps a quarter

of an inch thick. Piercing this top layer, I have run my arm down to the shoulder (about three feet down) and have found a black, tarrish type of silt underneath.

I want especially to bring up some object like a stone, which has without doubt been hewn or chiseled by man. Our first few dives convince me that our bare hands are not equal to the task. The silt lies too thick, and, if there are any artifacts buried there, they elude my groping fingers. So, pick and shovels join the array of equipment. All the while we are diving in this area adjacent to the Qumran caves, we search for man-made artifacts

with these tools. But the efforts are to no avail —
the silt defeats us. Once stirred up, it hangs in the
water like a dense curtain, inhibiting motion and defying progress in any direction, so we finally give
up the digging. A later expedition with trenching
and dredging equipment will force, I am sure, secrets from the bosom of this Dead Sea.

However, we do uncover roots, limbs, and
branches of palm trees with our pick-and-shoveling.
These discoveries bear out what Pliny the Elder reported about this area in 70 A.D. He wrote, in his
book *Historia Naturalis*: "The Hessenes live on the
west side away from the shores (of the Dead Sea)
. . . They eschew money and live among the palm
trees . . . Below them lay Engedi, a town once second
only to Jerusalem in its fertility and groves of palms.
Now it is one more tomb. Next comes Masada, a
fort on a rock, and like the former, not far from
the Dead Sea . . . " This bit of historical and
archaeological reporting has served somewhat as a
guide for me, and now what we are finding apparently is substantiating it.

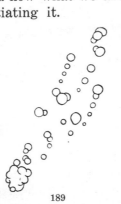

XIII JORDAN RIVER DIVE

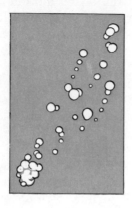

CARRIED TO THE POINT OF NO RETURN

March 12th is the beginning of another work week for the expedition. We have scheduled dives for every day in the sea off shore from Khirbet Qumran. A number of our yellow plastic buoys marking positions of several 'tells' were still floating and we are impatient to resume our exploratory dives in this region.

A flamboyant crimson sunrise meets our gaze as we look skyward to determine the weather this morning. But our spirits are not lifted by the glorious spectacle, as the clouds which add to its splendor are looming thunderheads. By seven o'clock the clouds are thick and rolling, then all the bottles of heaven tilt downward, drenching the land with rivers of rain. One by one we straggle in to breakfast, disheartened because again our plans have been delayed by a storm. These "latter rains" as the turbulent spring weather is called in the Holy Land, can become storms of fierce intensity. Having previously been caught out in the boat in gales of wind and rain, we find it wise to postpone any plans for diving when the storm clouds begin to gather.

Up to this time we have not made the progress we had anticipated due to a combination of factors, first being the weather. We cannot take the boat far from harbor in open water with high waves and strong winds. Secondly, the Moslem holy season of Ramadan occasions the closing of government offices and leaves of absence for holidays. We are frequently short-handed because personnel assigned to the expedition are gone "on holiday." So it is a slightly downhearted group which stands looking dejectedly out the windows at the soggy world that morning, wishing the clouds would roll away.

By noon our wish has come true. A swift wind from the Mediterranean sends the dripping clouds eastward. The tempest passes leaving only the gusty wind.

"Let's try taking the boat out, Doc!" urges my impatient senior diver. "Even if the waves are too high and we can't dive, we can at least make the run down to Qumran and check our floats."

The sailors are not too happy about the prospect of maneuvering the boat in the heavy seas this afternoon but after we outline our plan, the harbor master gives grudging consent and we leave the port, heading south to search for the floats. We find them without difficulty. Naim, our nimble tenderman, who is perched on the bridge and being soaked with spray every time a wave breaks over the bow, is the first to spot the yellow markers. We debate the advisability of diving, but as eager as we are to search in this area we feel is very significant, we decide that the risk is too great. We are cumbersome enough, hampered by more than two hundred extra pounds of weight, without trying to coordinate our movements with the boat and landing ramp heaving and rolling with the waves. We want no accidents.

Leaving the area, I instruct the captain to head the boat due east. If we cannot dive, at least we can continue our charting operations. Dean flips the switch which activates the Sonar recorder and we begin charting the topography of the sea bed in one straight line, ten miles to the eastern shore.

From the eastern shore we head north and record soundings along the shoreline. The terrain is very interesting here. Sheer cliffs project straight from the water, broken by deep chasms and fissures in the rock. Some small springs emanate from the rocks, giving fresh water to feed the Great Salt Sea. Further north along the shore, Bedouin families pitch their black goat's-hair tents, their herds of camels and flocks of fat-tailed sheep and goats forage on the scant gray-green patches of growth.

For a long time I have looked forward to exploring the mouth of the Jordan River. Being a student of the Bible, I thrill to the sound of the name, Jordan, and all it has stood for in those glorious, departed days. That the Jordan River played a significant role in the unfolding of Biblical history, there can be no doubt. So, the prospect of diving into the waters where Christ was baptized seemed reason enough for me. And, there was another reason for my desire to examine the Jordan River where it empties into the Dead Sea. I wondered where the 'line of demarcation' would be at the meeting of the waters. Perhaps I could discover the exact location of this demarcation 'line.' Perhaps the skeletons of too venturesome fish crossing the 'point of no return' would verify my theory. Soon, I will see for myself.

I want the captain to maneuver our boat into the mouth of the Jordan River. This proves to be too difficult a feat of navigation, however, as the Jordan disgorges tons of mud and silt into the Sea, making it almost impossible to find a channel deep and wide enough for a craft of this size to pass through. We have no desire to run this cruiser belonging to the Royal Jordanian Navy aground, so give it up and anchor in deeper water. The sailors and Jabra untie the dinghy, lower it into the water and we row to shore. Dean elects to stay on board, while I alone decide to explore the meeting of these two historical waters. Jabra and I, carrying my diving gear, walk from the mouth of the Jordan up

along its muddy banks, what seems a long weary distance. The sailors follow in the dinghy, straining to row against the Jordan current. Since I would be diving alone in the river, I want the sailors to be nearby observing my bubbles. They make slow progress rowing upstream, however, and finally pull to the side where one of the sailors catches hold of the branch of a small tree growing on the bank. From this vantage point the men can follow my progress under water and, I hope, will be able to come to my rescue if I should get into trouble underwater, fail to surface, or to make it to the opposite shore.

A single tank of air, face mask and regulator, knife, fins and depth gauge is all the equipment I have brought along—no weights. It is a relief not

to be encumbered with two hundred pounds of weights. Jabra helps fasten the straps of my tank, and I spit on the glass of my mask to clear the fog. Carrying only one tank of air, I feel surprisingly light and agile. I make a move to enter the water and find that I cannot proceed. My legs are stuck; I have to fight to lift them. Quicksand! And I have picked this spot to start my dive! Exerting all the strength I can muster, I manage to free my legs; they come free with an ominous sucking sound. Fighting and struggling, I finally get clear of the quicksand and dive into the water.

The visibility is not good because of the sediment continually being brought downstream in the rushing current. The water feels refreshing though, in contrast to the oily feel of the Dead Sea water. I try swimming underwater for a short distance, but find the current quickly takes me downstream. Diving down I grab for anything solid I can find on the bottom. I claw into the mud and rocks. Mud swirls around me but with a mighty effort I manage to pull myself along until I feel my strength ebbing. Flattening my body against the bottom, I clench my mouthpiece tightly between my teeth to avoid its being torn from my face, not moving until I can be sure my breathing is regular. Small stones being carried downstream by the force of the water make clinking sounds as they hit my tank. Bits of debris sting my body as if I were in a sandstorm.

I see a few wandering carp and cat fish swimming. If they pass the point of no return they will soon die in the Dead Sea's sulphurous, salty witches' brew. We have seen some which had been washed up on the shore as we were getting out of the dinghy, what now seemed hours ago. Indeed, there was a very definite 'line of demarcation'—a point of no return.

Reaching the bank, I am exhausted. I fling off my tank and lie flat on the muddy bank, inert, eyes closed. Brown waters churn at my feet and for a little while I am oblivious to time. The breeze rustles through the leaves of the brush growing along the bank. Suddenly there is another kind of rustling, the sound of flapping wings. Over head and flying in to land is a flock of wild ducks. I count between forty-five and fifty of them as they feed along the river's edge, unmindful of my presence. Those who say that there is no wild life around the Dead Sea are very wrong. Wild creatures abound in the "jungle" of the Jordan valley. Storks are frequently seen as they stop here to feed during their annual spring migration from the Middle East to Europe. I have even watched sea gulls drifting on the swells of the Dead Sea.

The sailors have seen me emerge from the river to rest. Now they are growing weary of holding their dinghy against the fast-flowing current and are calling to ask when I will start back. My answering shout, "Stay there, I am coming now," frightens the flock of ducks which take off into the wind, protesting loudly.

Entering the water again I examine the bottom more closely. It is a mixture of gravel and mud. Here and there are good sized rocks. I cling to one in order to read my depth gauge. It indicates a depth of only fifteen feet. This is the lowest reading. I let the velocity of the water carry me toward the Sea. The farther I go, the more difficult it is to swim along the bottom. I am nearing the "point of no return". Sweeping past a small tree, I catch a branch and hold tightly for a few minutes to examine its character and the bottom once more. Here I realize the fresh water of the Jordan is dissipating into the Dead Sea's brackish, briny cauldron. I no longer maintain neutral buoyancy. As I cling to the tree my feet swing upward, drawn to the surface.

Releasing my hold, I shoot upward, right myself and look around to see how far out into the sea the current has taken me. To my surprise I am about four hundred yards from shore. The dinghy is behind me but the sailors are having trouble. The erratic current is swinging the small boat in every direction except the one the sailors want to go. Our cruiser is a considerable distance away but Dean has seen me. The captain has pulled up anchor, started the motors and the craft is heading in my direction. I don't have the strength to swim very far so just float waiting for them to come alongside and pick me up.

The landing ramp being lowered into the water toward me looks like a long wooden tongue. I am ready to be lapped up onto the deck, you may be sure. My dive into the murky waters of the historic Jordan has not been deep, exhausting yes, but also rewarding. I am glad to get into some warm clothing and have a bracing, hot cup of coffee.

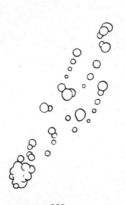

XIV OPERATION CORING

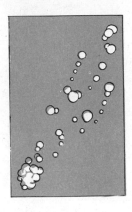

PIPELINE TO HISTORY

In these days of operations in the Qumran area, excitement at each new development spurred us on. Every morning the crew trooped to the boat and set out with dedication to our purposes secure in their hearts. Most of the time we were able to go straight to the areas planned for that day, but on a few occasions the plans were thwarted. When target-practice took over the Qumran area, or storms precluded charting or diving, rather than wait around doing nothing, I noted the most likely spot for exploration near the Dead Sea Hotel out of range of the aforementioned obstacles.

I refer to an island about six hundred yards out and directly in front of the Dead Sea Hotel. It is the only island in the entire Dead Sea. This fact alone was enough to excite my curiosity and stir up visions of historical activity there.

In size it is approximately two hundred and fifty feet long east and west, and one hundred and seventy five feet long north and south, somewhat the shape of an egg. Its highest point is about five and one half feet above the present water level. For long centuries, the island was apparently inundated. Due to the gradual fall of the Dead Sea during the past one hundred years, it has become visible.

One morning, being stymied in further exploratory attempts at Qumran, I informed the captain that I wished to investigate the island that day on foot. Up anchor and out to the 'egg' we go. Stopping just short of it, I have a sailor row me over in a dinghy. After a close inspection, I find a number of interesting things, signal for Dean to come over, and we spend some time giving it a thorough going over together.

The surface is covered with boulders and large rocks. Several of the larger rocks show definite signs of having been chiseled by early-day stone masons. We come across footings or foundations of various rooms at one spot. There seem to be three different rooms here, forming an L-shaped building. The lines are quite definite; we can follow the contour and arrangement of the stones which are obviously laid in that form. The whole

arrangement gives every appearance of being part of a wall or some type of building. One can only guess at the meaning of this construction. Perhaps in ancient times, there was a castle or fortress on the island. If so, surely there must have been access to the island from the shore, and not only by boat. If the island had stood high enough out of the water to have buildings on it, there should have been a roadway of some sort leading to it from the shore.

I decide the idea merits action, so, informing the captain of my notion, I have him circle the island carefully with the Sonar turned on. Sure enough, the charts pick up traces of a raise about three to five feet under the surface and all the way to the mainland on a northeastern course. Since this causeway or roadway lies in such shallow water, we gear up and go down to investigate.

But, although my hands tell me there is a pathway there, true evidence will have to be obtained through coring. I decide to test, in this spot, the device I have invented for this purpose in the Dead Sea. If it works as I think it should, I will take back to the States proof positive of our findings. And some day, I will come back to this island and roadway, sink shafts, and establish its earlier identity beyond doubt.

I have given much thought to experimenting and perfecting the instrument I will use as a coring device. Actually, it works on a pile-driving principle. There are three main sizes of pipes; the largest six inches in diameter; next larger, four inches in diameter; the smallest two inches in diameter. When threaded together, they look like a giant telescope. The largest one has a hard-steel cutting ring encircling the unthreaded end. A collar at the other end receives the drop-hammer blows, driving the whole telescoped pipe down and into the sea bed.

The complete coring device works this way: The largest pipe is lowered to the bottom, and a diver goes down to place and steady it. As the next size pipe, supported by ropes and cables comes down to him, the diver threads it into the larger one. The smallest one is then lowered and fitted in the same way with its upper end above the water. The hammer, weighing approximately one hundred pounds, is built on a special circular metal ring. When four men pull it up by ropes, winch fashion, to a distance of six feet and let it drop down on the pipe collar, it literally pounds the entire telescoped device down into the sea bed. The muffled pounding is quite noticeable to the diver below; sound carries through water extremely well. When the coring device is loosened and pulled up, its core is removed from the embedded end for analyzing and inspection for bone fragments, small objects, pottery fragments, coins, or other artifacts from earlier civilizations. The inner contents of this core were then removed and sealed in moisture-proof cylindrical containers to become the first specimens of our expedition for analysis in oceanography laboratories in the States. On the first test, my coring invention worked beautifully. In fact, the men were having so much fun with it, that before I could stop them, we discovered they had driven it half way to 'China'.

Now, the time has come to test it under actual Dead Sea conditions. After inspecting the island and roadway, I tell the captain to anchor the boat securely over the precise spot I choose for the first coring operations in the roadway. He drops three anchors, one on the bow and two at right angles from the stern to hold the boat steady.

With the coring device hooked up, we put it into the water without difficulty. When it hits bottom, it sinks a few inches, then the hammer goes to work. After many poundings, we halt the operation, and on inspection, the pipe appears to be solidly stuck. To finally get it loose, I go under, tie strong ropes close to the sea bed, then hook the ropes to the boat. I climb back into the boat with its two diesel engines and signal the captain to start 'rocking the boat,' so to speak. He starts the boat off in one direction, giving the embedded pipe a pull and a jerk, then switches to the opposite direction for another pull and jerk. Even with the powerful engines, it takes almost an hour of this maneuvering to work the pipe loose from the bottom and get it out. Yes, the device works, almost too well. Now, we are set to return to the Qumran area and dig into those 'tells'.

Revisiting the 'tells' at Qumran, we take cores from all, but we make a special effort at the largest 'tell', the one on the banks of the Wadi. The coring device is sunk squarely into the center of it. This 'tell', on an earlier exploratory dive, appears quite prominent. The very tip-top has a U-shape. I envision this as the tower area of perhaps a fortress or ancient city. The two tip-tops are the walls of the tower, I believe. In between, the silt is very deep. One can conjecture that the roof or ceiling has collapsed, falling into a room. I am anxious to sink a core here to see if my hypotheses are well-founded.

In such a coring operation, it is necessary for one of us to be down on the sea bed and the other on board ship at all times to direct the proper position for the driving of the core perpendicularly into the sea floor. The core goes in, all right. But once we had driven it to specified depths, the trouble starts. Here, as at the island it becomes so firmly embedded, we have difficulty removing it. This time, however, an hour and a single boat's rocking hardly makes it stir. No, it is two days later, with the placing of two boats in strategic positions, much pulling and hauling, and a worn-out crew, before the device finally lets go its hold on the bottom. The Dead Sea obviously does not give up its secrets willingly.

The first day trying to free it, the captain rocked the boat so hard, the cables broke. In the meantime, the sea took a hand on its own. Waves threatened to engulf us, so we decided to head for port and return the next morning, weather permitting, with both boats and try it again.

On the following day, we maneuver the two boats so that the core is between them. Then, attaching new cables to it and making sure the boats are well anchored, we try loosening it again. No luck except bad. This time the top section of the core breaks, leaving the main core still buried in the bed of the sea. Cables remain tied to it, so we station the boats in line with each other, anchor them, attach new cables, and this time, use a hand-powered winch of my own invention. Slowly, oh so slowly, the core inches its way out of the sea floor. Finally, it comes loose, almost causing the boats to collide. But, fortune favors us at last, and an accident is averted.

Later on, at the roadway extending out from the peninsula where the water is only five feet deep, we used the sledge-hammer to drive the shaft until it hit solid stone. At this point, repeated efforts were to no avail. Stymied, we could go

In shallow areas a sledge hammer was used to drive our coring device into the sea bed.

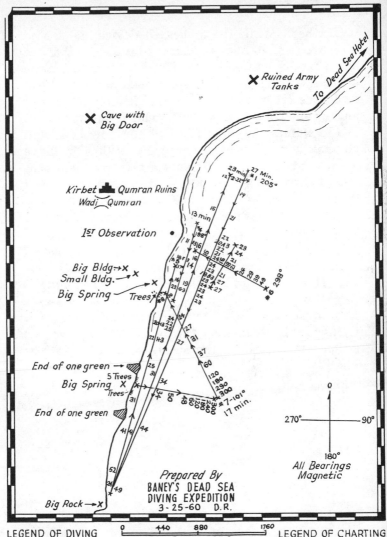

To Dead Sea Hotel

✕ Ruined Army Tanks

✕ Cave with Big Door

Kirbet Qumran Ruins
Wadi Qumran

1ST Observation   ●

Big Bldg.→✕
Small Bldg. → ✕
Big Spring → ✕
Trees

End of one green → 🢒
5 Trees
Big Spring ✕
Trees

End of one green 🢒

Big Rock → ✕

0
270° ——————— 90°
90°

180°
All Bearings
Magnetic

Prepared By
BANEY'S DEAD SEA
DIVING EXPEDITION
3-25-60   D.R.

LEGEND OF DIVING

E.D. = Exploratory Dives
P.D. = Pinpoint Dives
Ph.D.= Photographic Dives

0   440   880   1760
SCALE IN YARDS
0 to 60 = 4 Foot Variations
LEGEND OF COREING
C.O. = Core Operation
Red = E-3 Etc. = Corresponding
Locations on SONAR CHART.

LEGEND OF CHARTING

CSBT= Charting Sea Bed Topography
IRCT= Irregular Contour Topography
IPT= Indication of Promising Tell
BOAT SPEED - 8 KNOTS

no further. While the makeshift device had served its purposes, it had so many limitations that on our next expedition we will bring with us more efficient coring and trenching machinery to collect evidences from deeper areas. With relief we up-anchor and chug back to port. Our main work here in the Qumran area is finished for now, although not nearly enough has been done. What we have discovered here so far is only a teaser. I am convinced there is enough in this area to merit several future expeditions, because we have found the sea floor here literally covered by evidence of ancient civilizations.

Now that our work in this area is complete I will make my first report to the Minister of Education, His Excellency Sheikh M. S. Shanquiti, and the Department of Antiquities. A map of the area with drawings made by our cartographer, Mrs. Ryther, will accompany the report. Then we can go on to the other major location for exploration: The Lisan area.

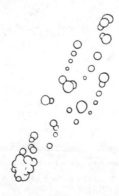

XV ENCAMPMENT AFLOAT

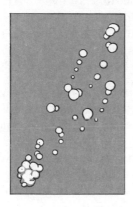

LIVING ON THE SEA OF DEATH

To make charting runs of the Lisan cove area, and subsequent diving operations, we were faced with the problem of locating a proper base in the same general area. Our earlier trip through Karak to Lisan had convinced us that the shore of the peninsula could not be used for this purpose, being completely barren, rocky and shadeless. Yet, to continue our operations all the way from the Naval base at the northern end of the Dead Sea would be impractical. The time used every day just to get to the southern end would be wasted; the five hours daily could be used more advantageously to complete the expedition as soon as possible. With the heat of on-coming summer moving in on us, time became even more of a factor than ever. Also, with the sea subject to so many moods, every trip from the northern to the southern end could be delayed by high winds and storms, and the days of charting, diving, or coring would thus be lost.

Since the base camp could not be established ashore, Dean and I discussed the possibility of operating from aboard ship, anchored somewhere in that area. Recalling the cove at Lisan where the two hulks lay rotting in the sun, we decided to use them as stationary bases together with our landing craft. Our cruiser, already outfitted with Sonar and equipment for diving and coring, would anchor nearby at night; during the day, of course, it would be used for our operations. So, we planned the moving of equipment and supplies with this aim in mind.

However, the best laid plans . . . . Delay became the order of the day. The landing barge needed repairs before we could take her down to Lisan, supplies and fuel had to be secured before transporting to the hulks in the cove; we all needed rest after the strenuous days of work in the Qumran area. All in all, four days were to elapse before the operations could begin from our base camp at Lisan.

In order to fully utilize the four days, Dean and I arose at daybreak each morning, rousted out the captain and crew, and made Sonar runs over practically all of the northern and eastern sections of the Dead Sea. In this way, the trips of five hours down and back were put to valuable use. This charting began at the island, then eastward to the mouth of the Jordan River, and following the eastern shoreline all the way south to the Lisan peninsula. On reaching the peninsula, bearings were taken at a point one thousand yards out and north, northeast of the point of the 'tongue.' Then, the plowing of watery furrows, back and forth kept us occupied 'til twilight, at which time we made boat tracks back to the Naval base at the northern end of the Sea.

During these four days the charting took place rather routinely. However, the weather was one unpredictable factor. High waves and wind also played a part in making the Sonar work less than routine. Buffeting caused mishaps to the boat, and sometimes the crew (and I) tired of battling the elements. But, the work continued in spite of the temporary handicaps, and was completed to our satisfaction.

At 4:30 one morning in the middle of March, Jabra, our expedition cook, arouses me with a knock at the door. I immediately throw open the shutters to see if this is a day when we can take the boat to the Lisan area. Several days of bad weather have prevented our diving. Even so, we hope to spend the day sounding and charting the topography of a special section of the Lisan area. A peek at the sky, however, reveals that to the south leaden clouds are massing. Still, hoping only a spring shower is in the offing, I gather the crew and we eat breakfast quickly. Jabra packs a lunch, and we reach the port just after six o'clock.

This Sea has more moods than an octopus has tentacles, each one changing like a woman's whim. Sometimes it is still as death, the winds subside, and the fiery sun quickly dehydrates the person foolish enough to be near it uncovered. But, then the gales come screaming from the south, the heavy clouds menace, the thundering gray waves pound at the beaches, and the salt spray angrily stings the face. In the spring, especially, the Sea switches moods like a maiden in love. This day we are hoping the tempestuous seas will calm as the morning wears on.

I instruct the captain to get the boat ready. "I do not advise you to take the boat out in this wind, Dr. Baney," he declares. I insist the morning storm will subside and ask permission to take the boat for a charting run to Lisan. He is hesitant, but finally agrees, insisting that the escort boat must go along.

We remove the landing ramp attached to the front of the boat; it extends too far into the water and would act as a drag against the high waves. By seven o'clock we leave the harbor, heading southeast into the Sea. The waves out here are much higher than I had thought they would be. The boat bounces and shudders.

"Sergeant," I shout to the man at the wheel, "steer a course straight to the eastern bank. The bluffs will break the wind, and we can follow the shoreline down to Lisan."

The prow swings to port, and we start across eight very rough miles. The usually thirty minute trip takes about an hour and fifteen minutes. Dean,

Dot and I are on the bridge of the little boat, clinging to the rail. Huge waves surge over the bow, showering us with briny water. Dean finally gives up and goes below.

Approaching the eastern shore, we are disappointed to find the wind currents have changed. They come now from a southwesterly direction. Thundering waves dash against the high bluffs, and the Sea is in a turmoil. There is nothing to do but face into the wind, hoping it will shift again. I am determined to get to Lisan and not defer our plans another day because of bad weather, so I direct the pilot to keep an even course about fifty yards from shore.

Our escort boat has been trailing two to three miles behind, and I notice it has slowed down considerably. We are moving around ten knots an hour while the other boat is running about five knots. Then minutes later, I get a radio call from the post; the commander wants to speak to me. The radio static almost buries his voice, but I finally get the message. The second boat has contacted the commander ashore and wants permission to return. I shout into the microphone that the sea is not dangerously rough, that our craft is riding normally, and request another hour to continue to Lisan.

"If the wind doesn't die down by then, I'll return," I yell.

I don't hear his answer. The boat gives a lurch. My head hits the sharp edge of the radio, and I fold to the floor, head swimming. One of the sailors wets a towel and sponges the goose-egg on my forehead. Some of the sea water trickles into my eyes. The smarting adds to my misery, but brings me back to consciousness.

The boat is really rocking and rolling now in breakers ten to fifteen feet high. No doubt about it, the storm is getting worse, but I hate to give up. Several of the sailors turn greenish under their tans. Fortunately, I have taken Dramamine and ride out the storm without getting sick.

A wall of rain ambushes us in a torrent, driven by the force of the wind. This craft is not built to withstand such a storm, nevertheless, it rides the waves adequately. The cabin room is so small that not all of us can stay below decks at any one time. Anyway, since the air is close there, we question whether to stay and be sea-sick or go on deck and be drenched. I stay topside until I hear the crackle of the radio again. I hear my named called, so I slide along the deck, struggling to stay aboard, and enter the pilot room below. The commander is shouting over the radio that we must turn back. The escort boat has slowed to three knots, and the crew is apparently threatening to return without us if we continue to brave the waves.

Between the roar of the storm and the shrill clamor of the radio, I make out the report that the Amman weather station has notified the commander that the wind is slated to increase in velocity, and the storm will not abate for another twenty-four hours. That does it! I give the order for our lead boat to return to the harbor.

Now, instead of hitting the waves head on, when

we turn the craft to the north we are riding the waves swiftly, as the wind is coming from the south. The crew is obviously relieved that we are heading home. Jabra brings our lunch, but we find it has been soaked with Dead Sea water and not a crumb is edible. We all stay on deck, enjoying the roller-coaster ride. The boat glides high on the waves for minutes, then plunges downward. The bow is inundated, and two men are kept busy bailing water, both in the stern section and in the bow, all the way to port. It takes us only forty minutes to return from nowhere, for that is exactly where we have been, much to our disappointment. Our clothing and hair are stiff with crystals from the Dead Sea water. Back at base, we sadly unload the gear and return to the hotel for showers. So ends a very unproductive day on the Dead Sea.

The following morning, this time under calm skies, we renewed operations. The charting of the entire northern end down to the peninsula was, as mentioned before, from the island, to the mouth of the Jordan River, following the eastern bank down to the point of the 'tongue'.

From the deck, I watched the short tableau unfold. Among the camels dotting the banks was one which captured my attention. There was a raven feeding on its back; the camel appeared oblivious to its passenger. As we continued the run, other scenes of animal life caught my eyes. In the distance, I glimpsed a small herd of gazelles, gamboling and feeding. Even a hyena loped along, cackling its crazy laugh. All the way down to the cove I was the fascinated spectator of this panorama of wild life.

The cove area charting did not take too long, but I was intensely interested in watching for results. Here, on one side of the cove, was one area likely to be a location for one of the lost cities. We made 29 runs here, working all day without taking time for anything but a hasty lunch on board. There was some important evidence indicated on the eastern side. Buoys were tossed out to mark these areas for exploration later. I too, have always felt that if we are going to find something highly significant it would be in this area, around the peninsula. The buoys were not too far from shore and right where the tributaries come into the sea. Also, there are a great number of trees in this area and the land is a quite fertile delta.

The sea was calm in the peninsula area the day we began charting there. Sailing one-half mile north of the peninsula point, we dropped our first buoy, marked "A", then took a direct course east, approximately two miles to the shore, charting as we went. At this point, the second buoy, marked "B" was tossed overboard. From point "B" we sailed due south, keeping about 100 feet from the shoreline in water from fifteen to twenty-five feet deep. We continued the shoreline charting all around the cove formed by the jutting 'tongue'. At the extreme southwestern point, we threw in another buoy marked "C" and from there we headed north, charting the bottom as closely as possible to the shore until we again reached our "A" buoy.

Point 1—The protruding tongue of the peninsula.

El Lisan's marshy shore and drowned forest.

We then continued charting in furrows, the area becoming increasingly smaller until, after 29 runs, the entire cove was mapped. We found the shoreline to be soft mud, but the bottom, especially around the point, was solid rock, covered with little or no silt.

The temperatures in the southern Dead Sea Basin were noticeably higher than in the northern section. We were beginning to look more and more like natives of the area every day with darkly tanned skins and wearing the local headdress, large squares of cloth folded for practical head coverings. Sunstroke was always a strong possibility, and working all day in the broiling sun on our boat which afforded little shelter made these head coverings a must. Two of our party suffered sunstroke, and the rule was made to have two or three sailors douse us with fresh water at intervals. The rising temperatures presaged soon-to-be unbearable working conditions; we would have to speed up operations or be caught short.

With the charting and mapping of the cove completed, the time had arrived to move our equipment, supplies, and the landing craft and set up our base camp there.

I got in touch with the Admiral of the Naval base—a fine, helpful man—and told him the procedures I would follow, the equipment I would need, and asked the number of sailors he could provide. He cooperated to the fullest and sent seven along, four to be on the patrol boat and three to remain

Two of the ship's crew on the top deck of our cruiser.

A derelict old tub serves as our Lisan base camp afloat.

Our cruiser and expedition party returning to camp after a day's operation in the southern basin.

on board the landing craft. With our own party of seven, this made fourteen on location.

The landing craft was ideally suited, after alterations and repairs, for coring operations and served as sleeping quarters and home base where Dot did her mapping work. It also served as kitchen and sleeping area. We took our meals there and bedded down at night on our mattresses. Our complete camp afloat was arranged in this fashion. The two large abandoned barge boats were at anchor about 200 yards off shore. We pulled the cruiser alongside the larger boat, anchored it, then pulled the landing craft to the other side. Then tying them together, we had quite a large walking area from one to the other, as well as a large storage space. The sailors ate on the upper deck of the old boat and at night, rolled up in their blankets and slept there.

Usually, after the evening meal we would sit around on deck talking. The mountains served as a back-drop to a peaceful but melancholy setting. Off on the shore Bedouin campfires dying down, the jackals howling mournfully, the baying of the tethered asses, and the short explosive laughter of the hyenas created an eerie sensation.

I had an understanding with the Admiral that when the supplies got low, we would leave the landing craft there with the three sailors aboard, and return on the patrol boat to the Naval Base. After replenishing our supplies, making reports to the Minister of Antiquities in Amman, picking up mail, cables, etc., we would return to our base camp in

the Lisan Cove.

    Living on these boats took on a primitive aspect. And nature added to our difficulties. By day, the sun made the heat and glare almost unbearable; then unexpectedly, more than once swarms of hornets would appear from nowhere, attack us for an hour or so, and leave as suddenly as they had come. We never found out where they came from, or where they went. At the times they besieged us, several sailors with wet towels would swing wildly to drive them away. And about an hour before sunset, pestering swarms of horseflies would put in their appearance, inflicting misery with every painful bite. The tribulations were borne with fortitude, nothing would sway us from our mission.

XVI ALONE IN THE DARKNESS

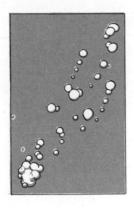

THE CRYPT IS MY FOE

"This darkness . . . this soul-stifling blackness
. . . is this to be my shroud? This blanketing, smoth-
ering, awful darkness, and I am alone!" The dreadful realization that I am lost and desperately alone
pounds at my temples. Unreasoning fear spreads
over my senses. My jaws ache from the strain of
clenching down on the mouthpiece. I dare not relax
them; one mouthful of this poisonous fluid at this
depth and I am, in truth, a dead man. My limbs are
numb; they have been over-exerted too long. The

stinging of needle-like pains in my legs alerts me to the fact that, besides the uncomfortable thought of not knowing just where I am or how to get out of here, I must again massage my legs or suffer with another painful 'charley horse.' And, I am blind! No light penetrates this gloomy cavern; my eyes, staring in agony, see nothing. Silence, the stark silence of centuries, muffles all sound except the frenzied pounding of my pulse and heartbeat, and the air hissing through my regulator. Is this to be the end of my adventure? Am I to perish here, down here in a tomb of my own choosing? How strange that would be if, through all my efforts in searching for Sodom and Gomorrah, I have stumbled into my own burial tomb!

What trick of fate brought me to this place? At what point had my calculations mis-fired? Where was Dean, my diving buddy? Was it really only a short hour or so ago that we plunged into these waters in high hopes and eager anticipation, full of faith in the success of our endeavors? What had gone wrong? Why am I now alone and lost in the darkness?

The questions gnawed at me. Maybe I could find the answers by reconstructing the events leading up to my being caught in the phantasmagoria of this moment. Maybe the retracing of steps in my mind would lead to a surcease, an untangling of the skein binding me in this web of cold, pain and terror.

My memory fled toward the track of the preceding few days, culminating in this watery prison

Approaching Wadi Mujeb, I study the terrain and wonder what artifacts we may find in our dives today into the deep chasm revealed by the Sonar recorder.

where I now find myself.

We were in the process of transporting supplies and equipment to the Lisan Cove in order to set up our base camp. During the trips down there from the northern end of the sea, where we had been staying at the Dead Sea Hotel, mappings by Sonar had been taken of the entire length of the eastern bank down to the Cove, and indeed the whole northern end of the Dead Sea had been criss-crossed again and again.

Approximately one-third of the way down from the northern to the southern end, on the eastern bank, was a location I considered ideal as the site

Wadi Mujeb—mouth of the Arnon River as it enters the Dead Sea where our Sonar recorder located the deep chasm.

for civilizations of another era. The terrain there had the requisite qualifications. Nowadays it is known as the Wadi Mujeb, a dried-out pitted 'valley' on the point of the shoreline, with the Arnon River flowing through it and emptying into the sea. The Wadi, in size, is roughly a half mile long and extends out from the mountains overlooking the Dead Sea about a quarter of a mile. In shape, this cupped-in area resembles an egg.

The Arnon River streams from a cleft in the mountains on the southeast side of the point. Its appearance makes me homesick; it looks so much like one of our Missouri creeks back home. The water gushes out with considerable force and at

A statue of salt-encrusted stone on a cliff above the Dead Sea dramatizes the Biblical story of Lot's wife who turned into a pillar of salt as she looked back toward Sodom.

this time of year it is almost half as large as the Jordan River. On the cliffs above stands a salt block resembling a human form. We naturally refer to it as 'Lot's wife'.

On the first Sonar charting trek to the Lisan Cove, as we neared the mouth of the Arnon River, the charts showed an extremely deep chasm. Vastly intrigued but, according to our timetable, unable to investigate this phenomenon immediately, we continued onward. The return trip to the Naval Base provided another opportunity to operate the Sonar over this area, and again the Sonar pictured the chasm. Each crossing and re-crossing verified the mappings and served to heighten our anticipation of what the dippings on the chart might signify.

Consulting with Dean, we decided to spend a day at the mouth of the Arnon investigating and exploring. Our curiosity was at fever-pitch, and even though I was anxious for our operations to get started from the base camp at Lisan, in a way I welcomed the delay. For, who could tell, maybe in this spot there was the chance to make that 'find' for which we were searching.

The plan was to arrive early, anchor the boat, then Dean and I would make dives for two or three hours to thoroughly investigate all the area adjacent to the Arnon and the chasm at its mouth.

When we reached the location this morning the sun was already bearing down heavily. The captain maneuvered the cruiser to a safe anchoring and we prepared for the day's operations from the landing craft, a short distance away.

As we would be going into great depths, using twin tank blocks, and making several hazardous dives, our faithful technician, Dot, checked and rechecked carefully all the gear, making absolutely sure that each piece was in perfect working order before our first dive.

The day promised unbearable heat, so, fearing the possibility of sunstroke, I arranged for one of the sailors to go by dinghy to the mouth of the Arnon and return at intervals with fresh sweet water from the stream. The sailors doused us from time to time with the cool, refreshing water, and also used it to wash off our gear after each dive.

Suddenly we heard a new sound, and saw to our dismay a swarm of hornets headed for our boat, flying in 'attack formation.' We rushed pell-mell

for covering of any kind, while the sailors swung wildly at them with towels and an old shirt. Finally the 'squadron' flew away, leaving only six of the crew with painful stings. The morning was wearing on, and it seemed that all the elements of nature were defying our efforts to uncover the secrets of the deep. Perhaps an ominous portent . . . ?

Around ten o'clock, with the hornets driven off and a fresh supply of water aboard, we gear up and plunge in to investigate the areas adjacent to the mouth of the Arnon. On this first dive, the cove and point are to be covered. Staying close together, Dean and I swim out some fifty feet from the boat and submerge, both at one time, buddy fashion, keeping in touch as much as possible. Around forty feet down we come upon numerous small trees. The

visibility is extremely limited, only about eighteen inches to two feet, but I spy a small tree and motion to Dean to help me uproot it. We tug and pull until it lets go. Giving it to Dean, I gesture toward the surface and we ascend. Breaking water, I ask him to take it to the craft, then we will explore farther down and around. When he swims back we submerge and spend the next hour systematically searching the entire cove and point with the exception of the immediate area of the mouth of the Arnon where the chasm lay. We find nothing more of significance, however, so with air running low and being fatigued, we surface and return to the landing craft for a rest and lunch and to prepare for the main task: the exploration of the chasm.

On board we talk about procedure and arrange our underwater signals. It is agreed that we will swim together down to the opening, approximately thirty five feet below the surface, then enter the chasm singly. The Sonar has indicated a small, deep chasm. I am to go down first, with Dean following my air bubbles closely, but keeping five to ten feet above—the bubbles being a guide to my whereabouts. We were well acquainted with the dangers lurking in the deep and recognized the necessity for reminding ourselves of what could happen down there in an unknown world of cold and darkness. We knew from past experience on so many other deep and long dives in this Dead Sea of salt, that legs, arms, and lips become numb after exertion and exposure to this water. Lips swell from the tension of biting down on the mouthpiece, and also, there is the dread of finding oneself alone in complete impenetrable darkness. All of these things we discuss and so, decide that for safety purposes, the one following must never lose touch with the other's air bubbles coming from his regulator and bursting around him. Heaven forbid that one of us should get lost in this indescribable world below, body knotted in pain and helpless!

Rested and refreshed after a lunch of bread, sardines and hard-boiled eggs, and with twin tanks checked, we gear up again and plunge into the cool water. As we head for the bottom, Dean stays just above me. We swim downward slowly as darkness closes in almost immediately, until there is only a deep grayness from which the slanting rays of sunlight have faded. Reaching the sandy bottom, I suddenly come upon the chasm drop-off. Cautiously feeling around, I get the impression that it is a shaft. Flipping my fins and waving my arms carefully — the density and pressure of the water combined with the very weights I am carrying makes this tiring work — I try to determine just how large the opening is. Not how deep, necessarily, just how wide it is around. Stretching myself across its mouth, I am surprised to find the opening is not over six or seven feet as I am able to touch one side with my fins and the other with my hands. Dean hovers just above. I cannot see him but a chance touch of his fins assures me of his presence.

After circling the opening completely several times I pause in prayer for a moment, praying to God to give me guidance, strength and protection in this pitch-black darkness I am entering. Then, giving the final signal to Dean, and he in return answering my signal that all is well, I begin my descent into the unknown. My depth gauge is unreadable, so the only way I can estimate how far down I am going is by measuring arm lengths. Going down approximately fifteen feet, with Dean following closely, I finger the sides, hoping to find and dislodge one stone and bring it to the surface. I am thrilled to feel even depressions in the stone, showing what I believe to be the marks of a mason who had chiseled these stones at some ancient age in history. The stones are covered with three to six inches of silt in some places. In others a great deal more sediment has collected. I literally dig my fingers as deeply as I can. The stones are there! I can feel them! But I cannot get one loose. They are laid too well.

At this point the familiar twinges warn me of approaching numbness in my limbs, so I stop to massage them. Also, I have a fearful taste of the foul water which tells me I must concentrate on my bite even though my lips have already become swollen from the effort. Swallowing some of this water I could strangle easily. I wonder if Dean is experiencing these difficulties also. Looking upward I see nothing, yet I know Dean is there and I am thankful for his presence.

After massaging so that my legs no longer feel numb, I continue down the shaft. Running my hands along its sides, I find it runs straight up and down with a very heavy coating of sediment. In vain I try to dislodge some of the stones which feel round, some smooth and some chiseled, most certainly laid there by a stone mason. All the while I am certain Dean is following my lead. I hope he is more successful in dislodging one of these stones.

By now, engrossed in my hunt for a removable stone, I am hardly aware of the depth, or passage of time. My regulator and the rest of the gear are functioning perfectly, so despite the numbness of my legs I pursue my objective avidly, lost in the wonder of being the first to enter this shaft since time immemorial. My excitement mounts, and I go deeper yet, continuing to run my hands through the silt on the sides of the walls.

But now feelings of uneasiness begin to be

aroused. The bottom is not apparent, and the leg cramps are recurring. The walls seem to be closing in. When a trans-Atlantic airplane reaches a point of no return, the pilot must make a vital decision, whether to go on or return. So it is with me now. Shall I go on down deeper or begin ascending? Knowing Dean is feeling my air bubbles as they wind their way up the shaft, and wanting desperately to bring back real evidence of man-made masonry, or some artifacts dating back in history, I decide to go on down. Was this where I made a mistake?

Minutes pass. All at once the configuration of the shaft changes! It widens, and I am in open 'space'! I can no longer touch the sides of the shaft with my arms and fins. However, I am not too alarmed. After all, Dean is still just above me.

I estimate that having gone down into this shaft seventy to seventy five feet, I must be about 100 feet below the surface of the sea, and must have been down now about thirty to forty minutes. Still eager to recover a stone, I stop again to massage the deadness from my limbs and calculate a safe margin of time for decompression when ascending.

Ready again, I work my way down and forward slowly, when suddenly, I am pinned! My regulator and air tanks are wedged under what seems to be a roof or shelf of a cavern! Working carefully so as not to damage any vital part, I free my equipment from the projected stone and feel my way along. Only the scraping of my tanks on this roof now above me orients me to the fact that I have gone horizontally rather than vertically. Now the picture begins to form. I am under something instead of being in the shaft! I continue about fifteen to twenty feet and am still unable to touch anything in front or below me. There is only the feeling of having entered a cave and that there is a shelf of stone or masonry above me.

All at once the feeling of being closed in overwhelms me. This is the claustrophobia I have always feared . . . If I could scream I would! Self control almost leaves me. In this blackness the walls are closing in. The feeling of utter aloneness is indescribable. Hysteria threatens to constrict my throat and for an interminable moment numbs all my senses. I almost panic. How can I escape, how can I free myself, how overcome all the terrifying forces holding me here?

Thoughts churn inside my head and my breathing is labored, but finally realizing I must regain control to extricate myself, I force myself to remember other such experiences of claustrophobia I have had under water. I recall that it helps to think about familiar things. I count my fingers. Yes, they are all there. I feel my legs. Their touch reassures me. I conjure up pictures of the cruiser, the Sonar equipment, the dinghy, members of the crew. With each recall I begin to regain my emotional equilibrium and physical orientation. There, now, it's becoming better. My breathing is slower, my heartbeat less pounding. Thank God!

But, although calmer, I am still in a dire predicament. Somehow I must extricate myself, all

238

by myself. I rationalize that somehow Dean and I have become separated, otherwise he would be at my side at this crucial moment. I fear for him and wonder what has happened. But right now the thought uppermost in my mind is to find my way back to the shaft and get to the top as quickly as I can.

Edging backward and sideways, feeling cautiously with my fingers and fins, I find I must pause for a moment again and massage the circulation back into my limbs and around my lips to hold the tension on my mouthpiece. Then going forward again, I constantly fan my hands in front of my face to prevent the possibility of running into something which would knock my face mask loose. Among other dangers of the darkness, every diver has this fear of his mask or mouthpiece being jarred from his face. The waving motions become automatic in dark water. This precaution becomes doubly necessary in this chemical-laden water since one gulp would cause strangulation.

Will I be able to find my way out? Moving slowly, and prayerfully searching for moments which seem an eternity, I finally reach an opening large enough so my arms and legs touch the sides. Here again is the shaft! My prayers of thanks are almost audible as my heart leaps for joy. I come up the shaft in circular fashion, judging as best I can in this darkness not to ascend more than twenty five feet per minute to prevent the dangerous results of too rapid ascension; thinking also that I may meet Dean at any time. The way up the shaft seems

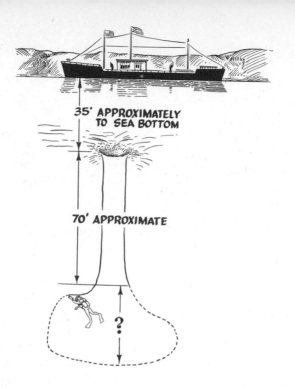

35' APPROXIMATELY
TO SEA BOTTOM

70' APPROXIMATE

?

never-ending and each time I stop for decompression, I try to picture in my mind the manner of place from which I have just escaped.

My over-all impression is that I had ascended into a long-necked, wide-bottomed pit shaped like a flower vase, so that the bottom of the shaft flared out into a bowl-shaped antechamber. This would account for my sudden finding myself in an open area larger than the shaft passageway, and also explain my regulator and tanks brushing the top of the antechamber.

As I work my way upward, the change from black to grayness alerts me to the realization that I will have to heed the pressures of the depth. My depth gauge still is unreadable, but I stop again to decompress before coming up farther. When I do emerge from the shaft the faint glow of light from above beckons me to the surface. I have no idea where the boat is. To orient myself, I circle the shaft. Knowing the boat is between the shaft and the shoreline, and taking into account the topography of the sea-bottom, I again circle the shaft to get the lay of the land, so to speak. My knowledge of how the sea bottom here changes in relation to the shore and going outward from it, stands me in good stead. The shore gradually declines toward the deeper part of the sea so, I follow the elevation working my way slowly upward. The shroud of darkness gradually shifts with the elevation so that the closer I come to shore, the better the visibility. The shift from blackness to grayness to a lighter gray guides me step-by-step into the shallower areas adjacent to the shoreline. At what I estimate to be a depth of about twenty feet I stop for the last time to decompress, and finally I surface, exhausted.

There, about one hundred feet away, rides the boat. Lined up at the bow, looking intently in my direction, are Dean and the sailors. As we spied each other simultaneously, they gave out a great shout of relief and welcome. I could only bob along, raising my arm in greeting. As I neared the boat Dean dived in and swam to me. Dean and the sailors helped me aboard and amidst a babble of greetings from the rest, freed me of my weights. I lay there on deck completely worn out.

As I rested, trying to recuperate, Dean peppered me with questions. Where had I gone? How had he lost me? What had happened? I was so weak that all I could do was say that as soon as I recovered my strength we would talk.

After a short rest and some refreshments, and with all aboard considerably calmer, I asked Dean how we had become separated. He said he had followed me down, keeping my air bubbles in view as per our arrangement, until suddenly he could no longer feel them coming up the shaft. Not realizing that I might have entered an antechamber, and thinking I possibly had decided to surface and somehow had slipped past him on my ascent, he came back up. On returning to the boat and not finding me, he became extremely agitated, put on new gear, and was getting ready to dive in and look for me when I appeared.

We discussed my experience in the shaft and the antechamber below it and decided that he must have lost track of my air bubbles when I entered the antechamber. We speculated on the significance of the shaft with its flared bottom, and I gave him what I felt might be a reasonable explanation.

At some remote time in the past, I conjectured, this cove might have jutted farther out into the sea and been a fertile area as evidenced by the trees we had found firmly rooted thirty five to forty feet below the surface. At that time, also, the sea might have been much lower than now, with the Arnon a

One of the interesting specimens brought up from the depths of the chasm area.

smaller stream than at present. Perhaps, I reasoned, this shaft and antechamber might have been a deep cistern constructed by the inhabitants of this fertile area (Sodom, Gomorrah, or another of the cities of the plain) so that the rainfall and water from the Arnon stream could be collected during the rainy season for use during the dry seasons. Dean agreed that my explanation had merit.

Later when my Sonar charts, exhibits and reports were examined in the States, it was believed by some archaeologists that perhaps this shaft and antechamber I had discovered might have been a burial tomb, as other burial tombs of apparent like

243

construction have been found in similar areas of the Middle East.

That night my prayers of thankfulness to God for my safe return from these lost depths sincerely expressed my relief that if the shaft and antechamber were indeed a burial tomb, it had not been my tomb. In thinking over the traumatic events of the day, my faith was renewed in that I had been permitted to continue my mission in life.

At this point I firmly believe I have come closer to finding evidence of ancient habitation in my deep dive into this area of the Dead Sea than anyone else in these many centuries. Perhaps unknowingly my hands have fingered not only the stone work of ancient masons, but artifacts, or perhaps even bone fragments in this chasm, cistern or tomb, whatever it may be.

On my next expedition, God willing, I plan to make coring, dredging, and trenching operations to the bottom of this shaft. I firmly believe that the results of these future efforts will be evident proof of ancient Biblical habitation lying buried beneath the waters of this area of the Dead Sea.

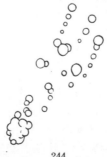

XVII THE SEA WITH DOORS

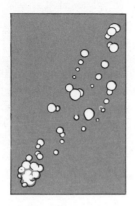

DETERMINED STRUGGLES TO UNLOCK THEM

With the camp arranged and fixed in place, Dean and I got out the Sonar charts of the cove. Our close examination revealed the exact areas we wanted to penetrate by diving. The peaks and valleys on the map pinpointed several puzzling possibilities.

Deep within the cove, not far out from our camp, was the first interesting Sonar marking. The depth here of only 15-20 feet made extensive diving preparations unnecessary. Going under, I found a rocky ledge, seemingly completely surrounded by mud. There was nothing here to indicate earlier civilization so after only a few more dives, we switched to the next area for exploration.

Just ahead of the ledge and heading out of the cove, the Sonar had sounded a rather large basin. On my first dive into this area, I came upon a real oddity. The basin—about 30-40 feet deep—consisted of fine particles of whitish, flour-like silt. Knowing I could not investigate this mass thoroughly by diving, since each immersion raised clouds obscuring movements and vision, I determined to search through it by some other means. For, investigating it to satisfy my curiosity had to be done.

Why this silt was of such different consistency and color from that encountered in other parts of the Dead Sea, where the whiteness came from, and how deep the basin lay were absorbing questions only closer examination could answer. To do justice to the explorations so that complete information about this area could be garnered would entail methods other than diving. Using all the ingenuity I could muster, I hit upon an idea. Would not a sled-like affair, on which Dean or I pulled along by the cruiser, do the job? This would give us mobility and, at any given point, one of us could stop and dig into the basin. We would have to arrange some signal for the stopping; otherwise, being towed 100-150 feet behind the boat and not stopping in time might result in a snarl of rope. Improper handling could cause trouble.

So, I invented an underwater sled. It was on

the order of a regular snowsled with runners. Of course, since weight was of utmost importance, I wanted it made of iron. As far as a guidance system, there were to be elevators similar to those used on an airplane. These would allow for raising and lowering; the boat pulling it would provide forward motion.

At the machine shop in the Trade School, I explained my design to Mr. Monsour, and he constructed it according to my specifications.

The boat made numerous runs up and down the silt basin, pulling one of us at different times, on the sled. It worked perfectly.

We never did make out why this silt had such a peculiar whiteness. And, as the basin extended farther out of the cove toward the open sea, the sled became useless. Below 100 feet, the tow rope was unmanageable, and as I followed the silt basin, the water here became deeper and deeper.

Incidentally, the sled played a part in the only near-fatal accident — and, indeed the only accident—I encountered in the entire expedition. On one of the dives in the cove, the captain was hauling the sled along at a fairly good clip. I was riding it and gave the signal to halt. Instead the captain speeded up. Fairly flying, the sled mushed through the water. Holding on for dear life, I felt a harsh mask squeeze. The force of the water almost ripped the mask from my face. Tugging frantically on the rope, I finally managed to alert Dean that I was in trouble. The boat stopped, and I started my ascent. When they pulled me aboard, we discovered that I had clamped down so hard on the mouthpiece, my teeth marks scored a ridge almost all the way through it.

On another day here in the cove, when the cruiser was laid up for repairs to one of the engines, and we decided to use the landing barge instead, Dean also had a close, extremely uncomfortable mishap. The diving was to take place not far from the base camp, about 200 yards out.

Diving from the cruiser, as we usually did, had created certain automatic motions in both of us. These motions related to protecting the face mask. Since the bow of the cruiser rode high out of the water, the dive would be from quite a distance and take enough time for us to set ourselves for the impact. During the short intervals between diving and hitting the water, reaction became automatic. The main fear was that the force of impact might knock mask or mouthpiece off with resultant swallowing of the acidulous brine, causing painful gagging. It is well known here that people do not drown in the Dead Sea; they strangle when the unbearably foul-tasting water causes the person's throat to constrict. Consequently, the one diving from the cruiser conditioned himself to involuntarily bring his arms close to his chest, pressing hands over the face mask tightly, and clenching jaws firmly down on mouthpiece.

This particular day, we used the landing craft for the diving. Unlike the cruiser, it rode practically flush with the surface of the water—about six inches above it. Dean geared up, jumped, and

before he could get his hands up, lost both mouth-piece and mask! From the expression on his face, I could see his torture. Brows knit, arms flailing, Dean tread water a good ten minutes, suffering until I could pull him out.

Hauling him aboard, I hastened to relieve his distress. We doused him with fresh water and poured 'bucketsful' down his throat. Ironically, in our desire to aid Dean, we almost drowned him. Dot, standing there wringing her hands, had almost as pale a look on her face as Dean. I heard her mutter later to him, "You scared me half out of my mind, honey. For my part, I wouldn't trade a perfectly good husband for all the finds in this Sea. Let the *Sea* be Dead; I want *you* live and kicking! You be careful!"

Dean coughed and spat all the rest of the day; diving for him, on that occasion was out of the question.

On other days, peculiar peaking on the Sonar charts showed possibly fruitful areas for investigation. The charting showed the Cove inclined toward the center at a gradual pace, dropping only a few feet. The Sonar picked up an interesting phenomenon at this point. Apparently, from about 5,000 feet straight out from the end of the Cove where we were based, a trough about 200 feet wide ran on out into the Dead Sea. The mapping of the Cove thus presented a picture of an inlet with sides sloping toward a deep-channel center. We did not dive into the trough; 'tells' or mounds were not indicated.

About the only other area of note in the Cove was a big forest on the eastern bank and extending for quite a distance underwater. Here, dives took us among trees far larger than those we found at Qumran. They stood close together, some only a few feet apart. I found them standing, seemingly petrified, in water 35 feet deep, and they were quite numerous.

I was very disappointed at not finding any 'tells' here, especially in view of the fact that not only our surmises had proved baseless, but also, this completed the work of the expedition in the Cove. However, I intend to return to the Cove and bring along trenching and dredging equipment. After all, that basin of silt and the rocky ledge need closer examination than we could give them this time, and

I believe some very fruitful finds will be made here.

But, I decide even better than a core would be actual photographs of this area. Here would be a very good spot to put to use that beautiful equipment we had obtained from Mr. Rebikoff's factory at Cannes.

Dean and I get into the water, and the cameras are handed to us. We begin to adjust their buoyancy. We add about four pounds to the movie-camera, nothing to the Torpedo Leica. We experiment with the Leica first; I tell Dean just how I want the pictures made: flood-lights converge at a distance of five feet and the camera aimed directly at that illuminated spot; and likewise with the movie-camera.

We take eight or nine different shots with the camera at various angles and distances, using different aperture openings, time settings, etc. Then, we give the movie-camera a workout. We do all this in depths of one to fifteen feet of water. Following this, we bring up our cameras, wash them off with fresh water, also ourselves.

I am extremely anxious to see the results and can hardly wait to get back to our dark room and develop the film. As it turns out, we have wasted our efforts. The negatives reveal nothing.

We try again the next day, but pictures are not to be had. The inescapable conclusion is forced upon us. The opacity of Dead Sea water defies filming through it, at least with the equipment we have with us.

But just to make doubly sure, and so that every

possible effort to photograph will be exhausted, we take the Leica and movie-camera on the boat for further trials. So that our attempts will be corroborated, I invite the best photographer in Jordan to accompany us. To expedite the photographing, a dark room for immediate development of the film is rigged up aboard.

Of course, the news of our failure to photograph under the Dead Sea arouses another wave of skepticism. I hit upon a stratagem to illustrate the impossibility of taking pictures in this chemical-laden water. I want no one to retain a single doubt concerning our efforts. Calling in several very good photographers to view my demonstration so that they can verify our difficulties, I have fifty gallons of Dead Sea water placed in a large glass fish aquarium tank before them. Then, holding a ruler inside and against the side facing them, I invite the group to take pictures. First, I hold the ruler inside the tank next to the glass. They take this picture. Next, I move the ruler back one inch from the glass and they take another picture. The third picture is taken with the ruler three inches inside the tank. When the photographs are developed, the first set shows the ruler plainly. This is the one with the ruler held against the glass. The second shot of the ruler held about one inch away from the glass shows the part out of the water clearly! The part below the water is barely discernible. The third shot of the ruler held three inches away from the inside glass shows the top part out of the water clearly also; below the Dead Sea water, the ruler is indistinguishable.

The demonstration serves its purpose. Now I can present indisputable proof that it is impossible to photograph beneath the surface of the Dead Sea.

Dean and I are still eager to have some good underwater pictures made with our own cameras, however, so we take another quick trip to the Red Sea for the purpose of comparison between its photographing propensities and those of the Dead Sea. While we were testing all of our equipment and cameras on our first trip to the Red Sea, we made numerous color shots. These films could not be developed in the Middle East and we had no way of knowing whether or not they were good. This trip we shot only black and white film which could be developed immediately.

3 INCHES
FROM GLASS

ONE INCH
FROM GLASS
1"

We work here for a day, diving down to 200 feet, shooting pictures along the sandy path between the coral bluffs and boulders. When these films are developed we see that our cameras are perfectly capable of functioning underwater. The pictures are good, and again we are forced to the conclusion that the chemical properties of the Dead Sea are the agents which prohibit filming beneath these waters.

Finally, after all these tests under different conditions, above and below the Dead Sea water and under the Red Sea, we regretfully clean up the Leica Torpedo and the Nautilus Torpedo movie camera for use now only in photographing landscapes and various points of interest above the surface of the

Dead Sea. This initial phase of our expedition must now be devoted to Sonar charting, diving and coring to produce proof of our finds.

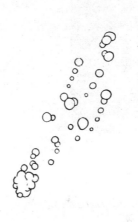

XVIII   STEP BY STEP

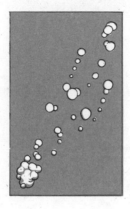

SONAR PICTURES: ROADWAY ACROSS THE SEA

The month of Ramadan was expected to end momentarily, with the first sight of the new moon. Ramadan is the ninth month of the Moslem year, shifting each year because it follows a lunar calendar.   All faithful Moslems, the crew of our navy boat had fasted throughout the month.   Fasting is observed every day from sunrise to sunset, beginning as soon as 'you can discern a white thread from a black one', according to instructions in the Koran. When Ramadan falls during the winter months, the fast is no great hardship.   However, when the sun sends its pitiless rays relentlessly through long summer days and dehydrates everyone in its path, holding to the fast takes almost superhuman will-power. When we were making our runs to chart around Lisan, crisscrossing the sea hour after tedious hour, the boat crawling at a rate of seven or eight knots an hour, on the days when we could have continued operations another hour or two, we put away the equipment and headed for port before sunset out of consideration for the hungry, thirsty sailors aboard. We were all glad that Ramadan was coming to an end.

Jabra, our cook, borrowed for the expedition from our Orphan Home at Bethlehem, awakened me one morning to say that we would not be taking any trips with the boat for the next few days. "The new moon was sighted last night, so today is the Ramadan Feast Day," he said. This suited me fine. The captain had forewarned me that all the crew would be given holidays for the Ramadan Feast. This would give me and our party time to return to our Orphan Home in Bethlehem to collect mail, supplies, gasoline, and repair equipment as well as transfer our Sonar chart readings to work maps for a clear picture of our progress and the expanse of sea bottom covered by the Sonar depth recorder and our dives.

The extreme southern end of the Dead Sea remained to be worked over. Dean and I decided that we would have to hurry or time and the unbearable heat and sirocco winds would put an end to the expedition prematurely. Consequently, we arranged

Point 1—The protruding tongue of El Lisan peninsula.

specified areas bounded by points of identification which we could chart, map, and explore in consecutive order until the whole area was covered. These points were designated 1, 2, 3, and the police post at the southeastern end of the Dead Sea on the Jordan side. We had to take into account the dividing boundary line intersecting the Dead Sea between Israel and Jordan and make sure we didn't cross it.

Point 1 extended from the point of the "tongue" down westward and southward to the farthest western point of the peninsula. Here we specified point 2. The distance between the two points was approximately twelve miles. From point 2 there was a small stretch of coastline which bent back eastward forming a small inlet. We designated the other

262

end of the inlet as point 3, marked by a large dead tree standing in the water. The remaining shoreline after point 3 led to the police post at the other end of the cove. These four areas, we felt, would finally reveal tangible evidence for which we are searching.

Having stipulated the order and areas of search, we now had to get ready for this last all-out effort. With the Lisan Cove area completely charted and explored, and the finding of the forest, rocky ledge, and the deep silt basin duly recorded, the final phase of the operation was set to be put into action.

I was greatly relieved when the last sailor reported back, and we were able to schedule the return trip to the Lisan Base Camp. We left the

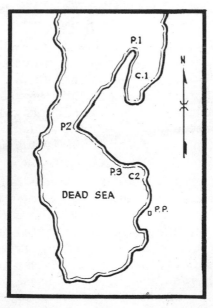

harbor at sunrise. It was a beautiful, fresh new day. We would not have many more in Jordan as the time for completing the expedition was running out.

Dean and I stood on the bridge, taking advantage of the crisp, clean air while the morning was still young. With calm seas we covered the long distance to the Lisan area in four hours. The last buoy we had dropped at the completion of our final run before going back to the Naval Base was located. With this as a starting point, we resumed our runs, traveling from east to west and vice versa throughout the day. Either Dean or I watched the Sonar at all times. It was fascinating to see the tiny needle sketching the profile of the sea bottom on a slowly moving strip of paper.

We even took turns eating in order not to waste time. The boat was equipped with a small galley in which the sailors could prepare their food. One of us would take the wheel while they ate. Jabra usually brought food prepared for us. Sometimes we detached the dinghy from the top deck. Towing it behind the boat, we used this flat top deck space as a table, or place to stretch out and rest.

For the next week our operations followed this same pattern as we made Sonar charts of the entire southern end of the Dead Sea. Our spirits were good, our hopes high, our determination undimmed by lack of time, weather or circumstances. Within a few days the evidence would be in; we would have successfully completed this first phase of the expedition. We had no doubt of the outcome. Every-

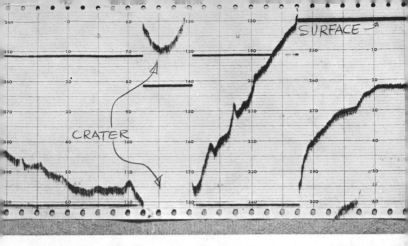

Sonar recorder draws a picture of a deep crater adjacent to the peninsula. The location of this crater lends credance to my belief that here was the core of volcanic action which destroyed Sodom and Gomorrah.

thing to date had substantiated my hypotheses and theories.

One morning, early as usual, we got the boat started on the run between points 1 and 2. We hugged the shoreline and turned on the Sonar. Charting steadily and plowing in the usual pattern, we made the runs back and forth out to half a mile until we hit deep water. At this point, the Sonar stopped functioning. Evidently this deep crater was beyond its range. In this entire area—points 1 and 2—we found nothing unusual on the charts other than a rocky crust around one point. We spent only two to three days in this area.

So little showed up on the charts that we didn't think it worthwhile to dive or use the sea sled. But

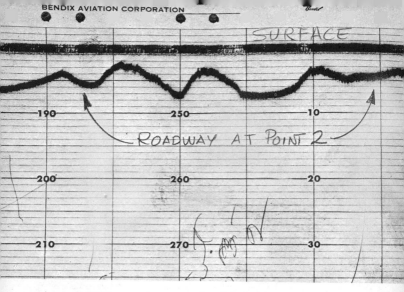

SURFACE

190   250   10

ROADWAY AT POINT 2

200   260   20

210   270   30

As our ship zig-zags across the dike or roadway, the Sonar draws its picture.

—rounding the corner of point 2, the story changed! Point 2 across to the Israeli-Jordan line of demarcation in the Dead Sea is a relatively short distance, point 2 being on a protuberance of the peninsula. As we sail around it, the Sonar does strange things. It jumps from an even thirty foot bottom line to only four feet! Just to verify this irregularity, I have the captain reverse the craft, and we criss-cross this point out to sea almost across to the line of demarcation. The Sonar shows clearly that whatever it is ranges from eight to sixteen feet wide and in length it goes all the way to where we have to be careful about crossing the demarcation line. It is only four to five feet under water, and we become very excited about this find. Contrary to usual procedure, I gear up and dive in to ascertain, if I can, just what the Sonar has located. Sure enough, there is what seems to be a roadway ranging from three to eight feet deep with drop-offs on both sides corroborating what the Sonar has told us. This is quite a remarkable discovery, and when I get back on board Dean and I discuss its possible significance.

I feel certain this bed under the sea is a roadway and reason so: in ancient days here in the Holy Land, perhaps this had been a dike. And when the Romans came, noted for their road-building, they had perhaps constructed a roadway atop this dike for the purpose of making a shortcut to Beersheba, Bethlehem and Jerusalem. Otherwise, the Legions across the Sea in this area would have had to march 100 miles or more to get to any of those places around the northern end of the Sea. In the next expedition, dredging and trenching will establish the truth.

Point 3 is marked by a large dead tree standing in the water. The distance from point 2 to point 3 is short, each run takes only about thirty minutes. Nothing of special interest shows up on the Sonar except the uniformity of the sea bed. It is apparently a continuous smooth bed of silt and mud to a depth varying from ten to twelve feet.

It is the area between point 3 and the police post which arouses our deep curiosity. This area is at the extreme end of the peninsula, and the contour of the land lends itself to my designating it as the Green Area since it is the only green oasis anywhere on this side of the peninsula. I had made an intensive study of the terrain in reconnaissance flights over it previously.

Due to the fact that this area was at the southern end, it came toward the last in our plans for underwater exploration. Yet to me, this general area was one of the most likely sites of the drowned cities. My logic for this was that the terrain here lent itself to the strong possibility that earlier the Dead Sea had swallowed up part of it. Above water at this point of the Cove is an oasis with tamarisk trees growing to the water's edge. (Evidently the underwater forest is an extension of these.) There are Bedouin tents, a number of small buildings, and agriculture of sorts being followed. The soil is loamy and the delta—for that is how it appears—is quite fertile. One could easily imagine this area in very ancient times extending far out into what is now the Dead Sea. The countryside is beautiful and green with bushes. Also, here, a perennial tributary, the Isal, enters the Sea.

All of my research and study, together with consultation with eminent archaeologists, had firmly convinced me that here, in this spot, was the location of either Sodom or Gomorrah. I had decided this area, rather than the Lisan cove, was more suitable. The topography of the region lent itself to my belief; here was a green area sloping gradually toward the sea to a depth of only ten to twelve feet with a tributary flowing into the Sea. This could very well have been a large plain in Biblical days; the volcanic eruptions and other God-sent manifestations of His wrath apparently caused the Dead Sea waters to rise and cover these lost cities. At no other place on the coastline of the Dead Sea could I find a more likely location where one of these cities of sin might have flourished and perished.

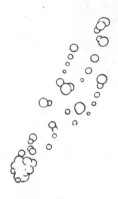

XIX WITHIN OUR GRASP

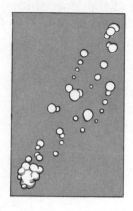

COMING EVENTS CAST THEIR SHADOWS

We are pressed for time. Our schedule calls for only three more days operations in the expedition. But before winding up our affairs I decide we must have a celebration as a memento of the whole expedition. It will be a farewell feast, prepared by Jabra — Arabic style — to symbolize the closing of my great adventure. I am humble at my success and deeply grateful for the help I have received from the crew. I know I can never truly reward these loyal, faithful, hard-working men for their devotion in the face of sandstorms, heat, sickness, wind and rain. They would not accept gifts, they are a proud people. No, the only fitting way I can show my appreciation is by a personal token of esteem. The feast is my offering of gratitude. I tell Jabra to make the preparation and leave nothing undone in this tribute to my gallant crew.

The next morning, at sunup, Jabra and one of the sailors rowed the dinghy to shore before I awoke. Already, I was making a personal sacrifice in the good cause; no breakfast, except bread and onions. From the boat, we could see Jabra bargaining with a Bedouin for a lamb. This was to be the main dish. Haggling for a bit, Jabra and the Bedouin finally came to terms, and an exchange was made. A fine bleating lamb was hauled away, tethered to a stake near the shore, and the two men began the process of cooking it. Taking mud and shaping it into a mound with a single opening in front, Jabra and the sailor built an oven, then cut the lamb's throat and skinned it. Soon the sun had baked the makeshift oven hard. After dressing our main dish, they made a fire inside the mound. Laying the complete carcass on top of the glowing coals, they then sealed the opening to the oven.

In the meantime, we had our charting work to attend to, so, leaving Jabra to his labors, I gave the captain the signal to up-anchor and start the cruiser toward our next scheduled area for charting. We chugged away, and I began to busy myself with the equipment. The crew was still a little uneasy over the possibility of storm conditions. The heat was overpowering, but I comforted them with the in-

formation that there would be only one more day to complete the charting of Cove 2 in the lower basin, and then we would all return to Jericho where the climate was cooler. The entire day was spent making Sonar charts of the extreme lower basin. We furrowed a good part of the entire area.

Late in the afternoon the sirocco wind hit us again, bringing the usual sandstorms. Limping back toward the base, we arrived at the same moment Jabra and the sailor were coming back to camp. I spied the grinning Jabra seated in the dinghy approaching. With the sailor tugging away at the oars, Jabra sat stiffly upright, a large platter bearing the roast lamb held high over his head. I'll never forget the sight nor the scurrying of the crew to help him aboard. A sense of good fellowship was

already manifest and the evening promised a wonderful time for all despite the sirocco wind.

When feast time arrived, Jabra placed the platter in the center of the deck. We all sat around it in a circle. Before eating, the captain and other top-ranking crew members, each made a speech expressing their gratitude for the fine meal in accordance with the custom of Jordan. I courteously responded with a short speech of my own telling them how pleased I was to extend this small token of esteem. With the formalities taken care of, the festivities began.

The platter carried the roast lamb on its center. Surrounding it were heaps of rice. In Jordan, this is a delicacy of the first order. Side dishes included onions, tomatoes, leban (yoghurt), and bread baked that afternoon by Jabra.

The Captain took a piece of the best part of the lamb, scooped up some rice, rolled the meat and rice into a ball and offered it to me, as the host. I took it, then rolled a ball and handed it to Dean, my senior diver and good right arm. This action signaled the others to start. Everyone started tearing off bits of meat, rolled them into succulent balls with rice and tossed them into their mouths. Amidst laughter and song, this procedure of "gracious" eating continued until the lamb was nothing but a delicious memory.

It was a memorable affair, and that evening with those fine fellows in the closing hours of our shared expedition will remain with me long after other incidents are forgotten. This was the most delicious meal of the entire expedition, as far as I was concerned, and not only because of the excellent repast. I could not help but enjoy myself. The hospitality of the Arab is unsurpassed in the world and that night I could do no less than reciprocate in their fashion, as the host.

All night long, after the feast, we tried to sleep, but only fitfully. The roaring wind — hot beyond endurance — and the stinging sand particles kept a constant bombardment on every part of the boat and us.

When we arose the next morning, rubbing the sand from our eyes, ears, and noses constituted the first order of the day. Then we braced ourselves for this last day's work, here in the deep southern basin of the Dead Sea.

The on-coming sirocco storm.

This isolated police post was one of our landmarks on the shores of the southern basin.

The captain and the others of the crew tried to persuade me to cut the expedition short; we had already charted all but one small part of the area which I considered most important. They were very uncomfortable, as we all were, in the teeth of the sirocco and the sandstorm. But I was adamant. The expedition must be completed. I reminded them again that the next day would see us back at the Naval base in the northern end; the prospect of soon escaping this heat and sand comforted them, and we started out.

This last morning we are completing the charting of Cove 2, adjacent to the Green Area, in the lower basin. As we finally arrive within 5,000 feet of shore in the region fed by the Isal tributary, we notice trees standing stiffly four to five feet out

276

of the water. The police post is about a mile farther along the coast. There are about 100 to 200 trees in the water about fifty feet from the shore. Where we are the water is very shallow, perhaps five to six feet deep.

This oasis extends only about 500 to 1000 feet from the base of the mountain out to the shoreline. The plain continues south and widens into a space filling about four square miles. On it are cultivated fields and a large group of palm trees. Almost bisecting the oasis is a tributary coming down through a break in the mountains. The water is channeled at several points into irrigation ditches divided and spread out all over the plain area. At the extreme northern end of the plain stands the town of Masara.

There are about 100-125 buildings in the area. They are small and made of brick and mud. Actually, it seems a typical Arabian village. There are some palm trees, and a few orange and lemon trees. The fertility of the ground is evident; crops of tomatoes, watermelons, potatoes, and other types of vegetables give living proof of year 'round tillage. The plain drops away from the mountains, and gradually slopes to the shore, inclining only slightly for the entire distance. I can see this whole Lisan basin is really a plain which at one time included the peninsula itself. The slope it forms as it leaves the base of the mountains down to the sea is really very small.

We chug along until we reach the spot where waters of the stream, Isal, enter the Dead Sea. We

are running close enough now to the shoreline so that we can see the Bedouins working their fields, with their flocks of goats and herds of camels wandering in search of forage. I estimate there are some 500 people living in this plain area.

The boat is running on one motor. The propeller shaft is broken on the other, and we are barely limping along. The sirocco wind overheats the equipment, and it is almost too hot to handle. The sandstorm pelts us with particles; the visibility is only a few yards.

We are only about 500 feet offshore at this point. Down to the water's edge there is about fifty feet of mud. We have a sailor taking soundings with a long pole to prevent us from running aground. The water here is only five to six feet deep.

We have been working all morning charting, and my disappointment has been growing as the hours pass.

I am watching the Sonar, listening to the drone of the engine and wishing I had a cold glass of buttermilk, when the needle of the Sonar gives a slight jump. It begins to climb the paper, straightens out for a 'moment,' then descends once more, leveling out in the same unvarying line characterizing this whole region. Quickly I take a bearing. We are near the east shore, close to the tributary. There are a considerable number of trees here, but this definitely is no tree! The 'blips' made by trees on our charts heretofore are insignificant compared to the size of the object now being projected.

I call out to Dean, who is repairing a piece

of equipment, "Dean, I believe we've got something. Come here and look!"

"I don't believe it," declares Dean, hurrying to see for himself. "What does it look like? How deep is the water?" His interest quickens as his eyes follow the unwavering line with its one definite hump, indicating a sizable object projecting two feet on the sea bottom.

Instructing one of the sailors to throw out a buoy, I order the man at the wheel to swing the boat around and make another pass over this location. Dean and I watch the Sonar in breathless silence. My heart pounds. Dean, outwardly calm, is betrayed by the clenching and unclenching of his fists.

As we come in line with the marker buoy, the

needle again climbs to match the protuberance below. We turn and run back over it to a distance of one hundred feet out and find it still continues.

"Dean, Dean, something this long must be a wall! Think of it! A wall! Do you realize what this means?" I pound him on the back; in elation, we burst into almost hysterical laughter. Here, on the very last day . . . !

When we calm down, by unspoken agreement, we rush to gear up. Even though the afternoon is wearing on, with the searing heat and the stinging sandstorm, we decide to go down. Despite the howling, strong wind, the captain is finally able to anchor near the spot peaked on the *Sonar* chart.*

This would be our last—our final—chance on this expedition. Next day will be too late. We

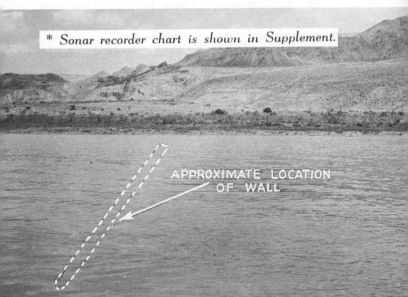

* *Sonar recorder chart is shown in Supplement.*

APPROXIMATE LOCATION
OF WALL

will not even be able to return later should we find what I hope for. Our fuel is running low, and commitments in Amman forbade any extension of the expedition. Even so, arrangements might have been made; but the sirocco winds were writing a period to any further plans.

Dean and I go in, one after the other. Entering the water, we find the visibility below matched by that above. It is nil. We are totally blind, so to speak. We locate the rise and work on either side of it. Our hands verify a bump-like mound running out to sea. We dig through silt and mud; it *does* seem to be a wall!

We work down here until the last breath of air is exhausted from our tanks. Then, reluctantly, we surface. The ship has drifted a considerable distance but we manage to swim to it without too much difficulty.

The sailors pull us up on deck, the captain has the anchor raised, and we start back to our base camp. The storm is still raging.

Dean and I lie prostrate, utterly exhausted yet exhilarated. Engrossed in our find, we are hardly aware of the repeated dousings of fresh water we are getting from the sailors. Actually, we do not want to be revived; the experience is wonderful and still real!

My conjecture is that it is a wall, I have faith it must be. For this wall, if truly it be, shows beyond a doubt that here is a remnant of one of the lost cities of the Bible. A wall, as opposed to a roadway, shows habitation. People, objects, artifacts . . . I have found what I came to the Dead Sea for! And on the very last day! When I return on my next expedition to dredge and trench the areas of my finds, this will be the very first.

Time has run out and we have nothing left now of this precious commodity. The excavating of these discoveries must now wait for another season. Besides, other equipment than what we have been using on this expedition will be needed.

That night on deck, by flashlight, Dean and I discussed until daybreak, how best to excavate these important discoveries on our next expedition. We decided it would take heavy equipment. We would require a special trenching piece which would enable us to dig furrows back and forth across the roadway and 'tells', giving us specimens from every part. As far as the wall was concerned, since it was in relatively shallow water, the trenching would give way to dredging if artifacts were found. The dredging would require entirely different equipment from what we had been using, of course. What I had in mind was to put a dike around the wall, dredge the water and silt out, then excavate it as dry land.

Of course the next expedition will cost a great deal of money. But with God's help and with the assistance of many who believe as I do, I will answer the doubters and prove the authenticity of the Bible's account of the cities of Sodom and Gomorrah.

XX FULFILLMENT

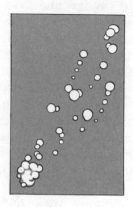

THE END OF THE BEGINNING

All these memories take but the space of a few quiet breaths. So much has been accomplished, so much remains to be done. But, the dream has come true. There in those turgid waters at my feet is the fulfillment, at least for now.

I come out of my reverie. ". . . . . . and we'll have to make the final report, Doc. Besides, there are all kinds of other details to take care of before we can wrap this up. But, it has been great huh? Hey . . . . . hey, Doc. Where've you been? I'll bet you haven't heard a word I said. Well, how about it? Let's get this sticky gear off and get going. How about it?" Dean was looking at me with a wry expression.

I mentally shook myself awake. It was hard to believe all the thoughts I'd had in those few short moments since he started talking.

Looking intently for a moment more at the peaceful scene in front of me, I turned to Dean and said quietly, "O.K., it's all over now. Let's get ready for the finale."

That night, after most of the packing was done and only a little remained for the next morning before breaking camp and heading back to the Naval Base, I broached an idea to my party.

"I think, as a fitting climax to this wonderful adventure, I would like to revisit each spot on this Dead Sea where we fought for and found the evidence to make this dream of mine come true. Standing here, looking out over the water and remembering these three months of our work here searching for Sodom and Gomorrah, I can conceive of no better way to put a period to our trying to ferret out the secrets of man in his journey through time."

A hush fell over the group. I could see they all were caught in the tug of personal memories, just as I had been earlier that day on the rocky shore. There was unspoken assent on their faces. They, too, shared with me in wanting to revisit the scenes of our triumphs and, also, of our hardships.

My conviction is that the ruins of the lost cities are in this area. Although they are buried deep beneath the silt that the waters of the Jordan and Arnon Rivers have washed into the Sea, I have felt them with my hands. I pray God to give me strength and the means to roll back the shallow seas from this Lisan basin area so I may excavate openly in the brilliant sunlight the evidence of these cities of Sodom and Gomorrah.

With God's help I shall spare no effort to uncover them, as I believe it would please God that, now, in this troubled world, man should pause long enough to remember God's willingness to accept the bargaining of Lot to save even ten righteous men from the fiery destruction of Sodom. Of course, Lot did not foresee the loss of his beloved wife who, in her typical feminine curiosity, refused God's word and looked backward. The statues of salt we have observed in this area of the Dead Sea stand as mute testimonials to her punishment.

The next morning we broke camp. Then, the last tour of the Dead Sea began.

It would be difficult, however, since the sirocco wind had greeted us with searing heat and pelting sand. But, there was to be no delay; commitments had to be fulfilled, and this must be the finish of the expedition. Although the visibility became increasingly poor, I wanted the captain to make the grand swing on the voyage back to the Naval Base to the places I had experienced the thrill of discovery. The storm grew in intensity, but I was determined to battle the sea, even on this last day. Amid an air of uneasiness on the part of the captain and crew, but a sense of anticipation from my own party, we set out.

Having spent the morning finishing up the packing and putting the Lisan Cove in the same shape we had found it, we did not attempt to revisit the southern basin of the Dead Sea. We were short of drinking water, the limping motor inhibited speed, the sirocco was growing in intensity, and we were anxious to get back to the Naval Base before night. Because of these factors we did not make the long journey to Cove No. 2 to revisit the location where, just yesterday, we discovered what I believe to be a wall—one of our most important finds.

Slowly chugging northward, the landing craft bringing up our rear, the scene at Wadi Mujeb

Returning to the Naval base, I dictate impressions of this last morning—the climax of our expedition.

brought back memories of the claustrophobia I had experienced at the bottom of the deep shaft. On up the coast we crossed over to the western bank and gazed silently at the ruins of Khirbet Qumran as the boat glided over those mysterious 'tells' and the forest. Around the wide circle of the northern end of the Dead Sea, we sighted the Dead Sea Hotel and the little island standing out in the water in front of it. I wondered if my theories about it and the connecting roadway would prove out. Next, we viewed again the mouth of the Jordan River. Then, we returned to anchor at the Naval Base. The tour was over, the expedition was done.

I had told the captain that I wanted to thank personally each member of the crew for their

Dean and I say goodbye and express our deep appreciation to the gallant crew who shared with us the toils of this expedition.

valuable services. At this moment the awareness of their contributions rendered to this expedition struck me forcibly. I shook each crew member's hand in deep gratitude. This expedition and its success would not have been possible had it not been for the patronage of His Majesty King Hussein, who made available to us the very necessary facilities of the Royal Jordanian Air Force, Army and Navy, and the services of the sailors who went with us in our search for the buried cities of yesteryear.

And I wanted especially at this moment to express my heartfelt thanks to both my senior diver and his lovely wife, our cartographer. Walking over to Dean and Dot Ryther, I gave them my hand in a clasp I hoped would convey my feelings. Dean, my friend and diving partner throughout this expedition and for years before, had been courageous and untiring in his efforts to aid me whenever and wherever we had dived. Never had I found him wanting in the virtues which are proof of a man's character. I sincerely hope that on my next expedition I will again be so fortunate as to have alongside of me this man, who so willingly and bravely shared with me the dangers of these Dead Sea waters.

On shore I was very happy to find my good and warm friends, the Ashours, and others, waiting to congratulate me. They were overjoyed at the successful culmination of the expedition.

Our whole party then went to the Dead Sea Hotel, where, after doffing my salt-stiffened clothing and luxuriating in a warm bath, I dictated the complete, final report to Mr. Rafieh, Acting Director of the Department of Antiquities.

That evening I gathered my closest friends around me—Dean, Dot, Vi, Mike and the Ashours. We sat there on the veranda, realizing it would soon be time for us to return home. There was little talk; we were sad, knowing that we were saying good-bye to the Dead Sea. In many ways the expedition had been a very difficult, tiresome operation, somewhat dangerous in many respects, and very uncomfortable at times. Yet all had shared in it uncomplainingly. And we all felt that the expedition had been a success.

So, it was with some pathos and a tinge of regret that we gazed out at the Sea. There was something about this Sea which was quite enchanting, yet she has been very angry with us ever since we came and began insisting upon her giving up her secrets. She has fought us tooth and nail; she will never truly befriend anyone trying to invade her private domain. Her weapons of density and heaviness allied with nature's storms will forever be her defense against easy entry. Yes, the Sea will continue to fight to hold her treasures intact, but I shall return one day and take up the cudgels again in the never-ending search to authenticate Biblical truth.

THE NEXT STEP —

To complete the underwater excavation of these ancient sites located on the first expedition. This book was written to help in achieving this purpose, and all proceeds accruing from its sale will be used exclusively for the purchase of equipment necessary for the successful completion of the second expedition.

A CONSCIENTIOUS DECISION —

The Baney Dead Sea Expedition is incorporated as a non-profit organization for Biblical research and marine archaeological exploration, with all derived proceeds to be used solely for the care of the orphans and crippled children of Jordan.

Feeling strongly concerning the plight of these unfortunate children on whose behalf I have labored for many years, I have resolved that any monetary returns derived from the success of my undertaking shall be utilized in services for their benefit.

Also, because of the most kind and generous patronage of His Majesty King Hussein of Jordan, my gratitude can best find expression in focusing wider attention on his kingdom, the hallowed cradle of the world's three great religions.

To portray graphically the procedures and equipment necessary to the next expedition, the following sketches will describe partially the tactics to be utilized. For the reader, unfamiliar with technical terminology, I have purposely written this book, and especially the descriptions of the sketches and operations pictured, in a non-technical manner.

ANCHORAGE OVER ANTIQUITY

Both houseboat and barge equipped for underwater excavation are stationed over the site of a 'tell' or wall pinpointed by a buoy. The flag of Jordan flies from the mast of the houseboat which serves as a laboratory and living quarters.

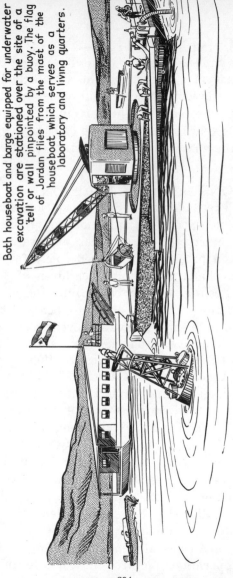

This sketch portrays the projected master plan for a completely self-contained operational encampment afloat. The equipment for locating, exploring, unearthing and analyzing remains of suspected archaeological sites consists basically of two sea crafts—a survey boat built in the form of a houseboat and an accompanying tender barge. Both will be securely anchored over areas believed able to render scientific data.

The major unit, the houseboat, will provide a floating home base with accommodations for fifteen to eighteen personnel. One section will be living quarters. Ample storage space will afford facilities for fresh water, foodstuffs, and other supplies sufficient to enable us to remain on location for weeks at a time.

From a technical standpoint, the houseboat will be powered by diesel engines. Other features will include a diesel-powered dynamo, space for an air bank, diving gear, ship-to-shore radio, a decompression chamber for emergency use by divers, a small machine shop, a laboratory equipped to analyze sediment, cores and artifacts, and a topography room where charts can be prepared on location. A landing ramp attachment, two Sonar Depth Recorder instruments (one a powerful Precision Depth Recorder to chart the sea bed at its deepest depths), and upper and lower deck walkways make the houseboat a unique floating headquarters for this next expedition.

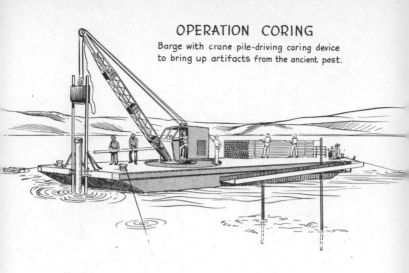

OPERATION CORING
Barge with crane pile-driving coring device
to bring up artifacts from the ancient past.

    With the barge securely anchored over a promising site, its crane pile-driving core device will go into action. This equipment will enable us to recover compact sediment and materials from deep in the sea floor which may contain evidences of earlier civilization. Analyzation of the cores should provide mankind with prima facie evidence of the ancient past.

    The importance of such coring operations will be found in the supplement to this book, "A Reconnaissance Study of the Floor of the Dead Sea", written by Dr. K. O. Emery, Professor of Geology of the University of Southern California.

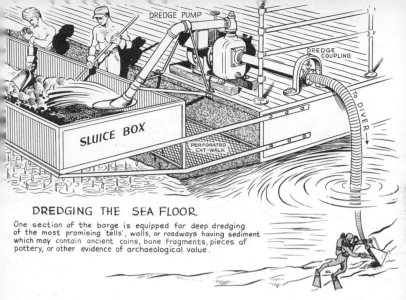

DREDGING THE SEA FLOOR

One section of the barge is equipped for deep dredging of the most promising 'tells', walls, or roadways having sediment which may contain ancient coins, bone fragments, pieces of pottery, or other evidence of archaeological value.

One section of the barge will be ideally equipped with a large dredge which has attached a lengthy flexible tube to allow operation in considerable depths. The dredge will serve varied purposes. First, over prominent sites the diver, as in the sketch, will guide the mouth of the dredge as it draws up sea floor strata which is pumped into a sluice-box where trained personnel will screen out objects for analyzation. Several hundred yards can be pumped by the dredge in one day's operation. Second, on a 'tell' or undersea wall or roadway, it will be used to vacuum clean and sweep clear the entire area for closer inspection to determine the direction for trenching or coring operations. Third, after a caisson is forced around a curious configuration on the sea bed, the dredge can be used to draw and pump the water out of it.

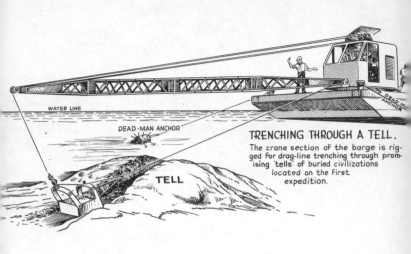

TRENCHING THROUGH A TELL.

The crane section of the barge is rigged for drag-line trenching through promising 'tells' of buried civilizations located on the first expedition.

The most important piece of equipment on the barge will be the crane adapted for pile-driving and drag-line operations.

The adjacent sketch shows the manner in which the barge and its equipment would be used to cut and scoop out a trench approximately three feet wide and quite deep through the middle or across a 'tell' such as those found on the first expedition in the Qumran area. The drag-line shovel would bring up the contents of the trench and drop it into the sluice-box where it would be washed and sifted for artifacts which could give mute evidence of habitation from the long-dead past.

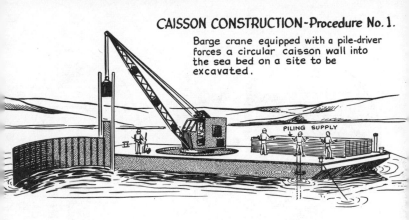

CAISSON CONSTRUCTION - Procedure No. 1.

Barge crane equipped with a pile-driver forces a circular caisson wall into the sea bed on a site to be excavated.

PILING SUPPLY

As described in the chapter "Within Our Grasp", one of our most promising "finds" was the wall in the lower basin area. The depth here is only about eleven feet, as shown by the Sonar and described in this chapter, as well as in the Supplement by Dr. Emery. Using the barge with crane and pile-driving equipment, we are assured it is possible to erect a caisson around the most promising section of this wall for open exploration.

After the exact location of the wall has been re-established, the barge will be anchored over it. First, we will use the dredge to vacuum clean the deep silt which surrounds the entire wall, thus providing the best possible underwater examination to determine the section of the wall to be excavated. We will next use the crane for drag-line trenching, cutting the wall to the desired depths in two places. Following this, a caisson will be driven to encircle an area of one to two hundred feet, depending upon the length of wall to be excavated.

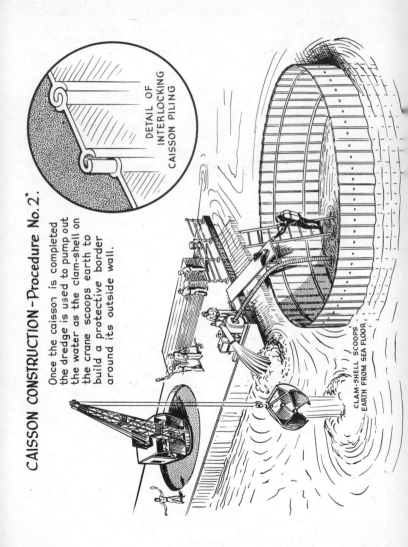

CAISSON CONSTRUCTION - Procedure No. 2.

Once the caisson is completed the dredge is used to pump out the water as the clam-shell on the crane scoops earth to build a protective border around its outside wall.

DETAIL OF INTERLOCKING CAISSON PILING

CLAM-SHELL SCOOPS EARTH FROM SEA FLOOR

As the sketch shows, the operation is basically the erection of the caisson which is constructed with the use of steel panels. Each inter-locking, watertight section will be pile-driven to desired depths. When the circular caisson is completed, the dredge pump will begin pumping out the water. Next, the crane, equipped with a clam-shell claw, will build an embankment around the caisson to relieve the pressure of water against it, and to lessen the probability of seepage beneath the caisson.

There will also be underwater intercommunications equipment to provide the transmitting of instructions from divers on the bed of the caisson to men on the barge and vice versa.

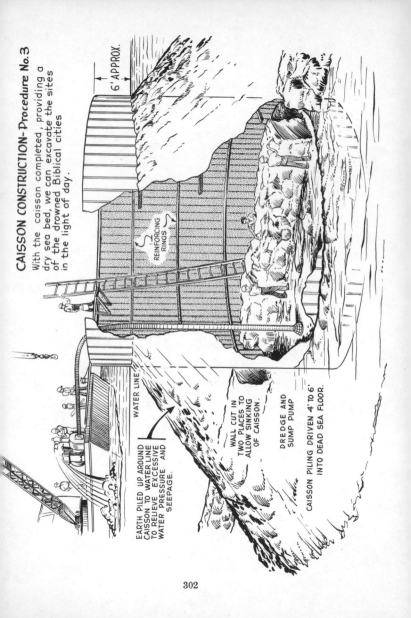

CAISSON CONSTRUCTION–Procedure No.3

With the caisson completed, providing a dry sea bed, we can excavate the sites of the drowned Biblical cities in the light of day.

6' APPROX.

REINFORCING RINGS

WATER LINE

EARTH PILED UP AROUND CAISSON TO WATER LINE TO RELIEVE EXCESSIVE WATER PRESSURE AND SEEPAGE.

WALL CUT IN TWO PLACES TO ALLOW SINKING OF CAISSON.

DREDGE AND SUMP PUMP

CAISSON PILING DRIVEN 4' TO 6' INTO DEAD SEA FLOOR.

When the caisson has been completed as pictured in the sketch, the water pumped out, and the protective wall constructed around it, a large area of perhaps one to two hundred feet in diameter will be laid bare. We can examine then, in dryness and safety, artifacts from the wall which I believe, without doubt, to have been a part of either Sodom or Gomorrah.

All of the aforementioned sketches show partially the procedures of the next expedition and some of our plans to unearth our 'finds'. Employing these various procedures, I dedicate myself to baring to bright sunlight what has been buried so long from the sight of man—since their destruction in the time of Abraham. On this next expedition I am most confident that we can reveal something of the culture and mores of those Biblical days and thus humbly verify the scriptural account of God's destruction by fire and brimstone of the wicked cities of Sodom and Gomorrah.

A RECONNAISSANCE STUDY
OF THE FLOOR
OF THE DEAD SEA

K. O. EMERY
University of Southern California

During the spring of 1960 the Rev. Ralph E. Baney of the Christian Approach Mission in Bethlehem, Jordan made a reconnaissance study of the Dead Sea floor using modern sounding and diving equipment. This equipment is so much better than that which was available to Lt. W. E. Lynch of the U.S. Navy for his survey of the Dead Sea in 1848 that Mr. Baney asked me to examine the results of the new work. I take pleasure in reporting them here, because of interest in the Dead Sea developed during and prior to a visit to it in 1959 during a brief tour of Jordan.

Figure 1. *Aerial view of south basin of Dead Sea showing its separation from the north basin by El Lisan peninsula. Photographed about 1945.*

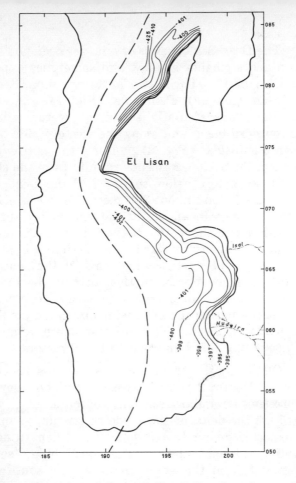

Figure 2. Contours of floor of Dead Sea based on echo soundings made by Mr. Baney during the spring of 1960 when the Dead Sea level was about 396 meters below the Mediterranean Sea level. Soundings by Bendix echo sounder were increased 15 per cent to correct for the high sound velocity caused by the high salinity and high temperature of the water.

The Dead Sea consists of a larger deep northern basin and a smaller shallow and sometimes exposed southern basin. These two parts are separated by El Lisan (tongue) Peninsula (Fig. 1). Most of Mr. Baney's systematic soundings were made in the southern basin and along the western side of El Lisan Peninsula (Fig. 2). Along the entire area sounded, the bottom descends rapidly from the shore to several meters below the level of the Dead Sea, which itself stood about 396 meters below the level of the Mediterranean Sea at the time of the survey. Farther from shore the bottom is flatter, but it gradually deepens seaward to a maximum depth of 6 meters in the north central part of the southern basin. Farther north, in the northern basin, one of the sounding lines fringed a steep slope which continues down to the 400-meter maximum depth of the northern basin. The greatest depth found on this sounding line happened to be 30 meters.

On the basis of all these soundings the contours of Figure 2 were drawn. They show several interesting irregularities. The contours bulge westward off the delta of the Hudeira stream, as might be expected owing to relatively rapid deposition of detrital sediment there. They also bulge southwestward from the small point at the south side of El Lisan Peninsula. A westward bulge from the westerly tip of El Lisan Peninsula is suggested by soundings, in agreement with the light-colored area shown there by the aerial photograph (Fig. 1), but unfortunately the position control for soundings in that area was not good enough to permit

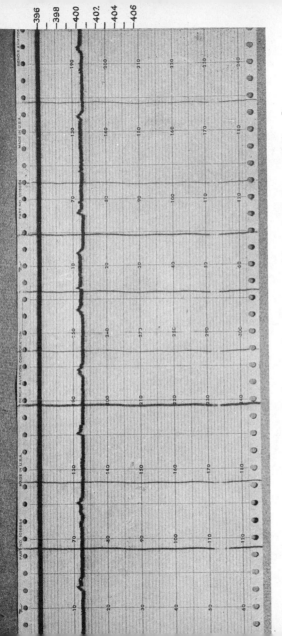

Figure 3. Echogram of bottom in northeastern part of southern basin of Dead Sea (diving station C of Figure 4) showing a possible submerged roadway or a low wall which was crossed and recrossed by the sounding boat on a zig-zag course (each course change is indicated by a vertical pencil line). Scale at left margin gives depths in feet uncorrected for sound velocity; scale at right gives corrected elevation in meters with respect to Mediterranean Sea level.

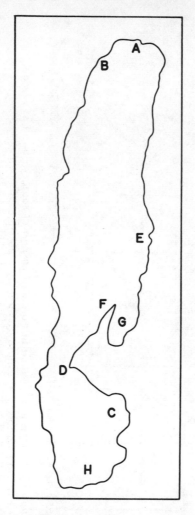

Figure 4. Diving stations occupied by
Mr. Baney during the spring of 1960.

the drawing of contours.

Of considerable interest is a small topographic feature which crosses part of the flat floor of the southern basin. This feature (Fig. 3) stands nearly a meter above the general bottom level, it is linear, and it appears to extend southwesterly from near the shore to the area marked C on Figure 4. It was crossed repeatedly by the zig-zagging survey boat. This feature has the appearance of being a submerged roadway or a low wall and it deserves future detailed mapping and examination.

Many of Mr. Baney's dives (stations B, C, D, E, and G of Figure 4) revealed the presence of small trees in growth position, at a depth of 7 meters means that at the time when they were alive the sea must have been low enough (—403 meters) to expose the entire southern basin.

A radiocarbon age for a piece of wood from one such tree was measured by Dr. T. A. Rafter of New Zealand. The wood proved to be modern (or less than 200 years old). Now, according to travelers' reports, the little island of Rujm el-Bahr off the Dead Sea Hotel at the north end of the Sea was exposed so high between the years 1807 and 1829 that the Dead Sea level must have been down to about —402 meters elevation, low enough to permit trees to have grown elsewhere around the shore. After 1829 the sea level rapidly rose. Confirmation of this low water level is provided by the stories of camel caravans fording Lisan Strait during the early 19th century. Thus it seems probable that the trees were alive about 150 years ago.

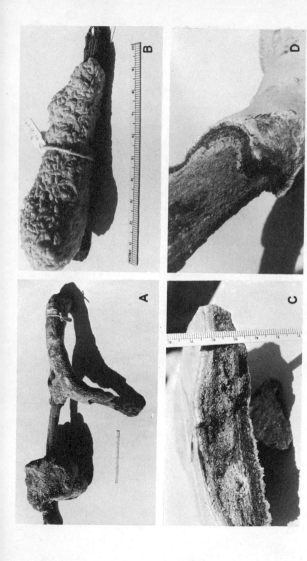

Figure 5. Photographs of wood and gypsum crusts recovered by diving.

Other low water levels probably occurred much earlier, but evidence for them is less definite. Among the evidence which can be cited is the discovery by Mr. Baney on one of his dives (station A of Figure 4) of a possible road submerged about one meter (to —397 meters) leading out to Rujm el-Bahr, reputed to be the site of a Roman fort. Also the famous medieval Madaba map shows only a single basin, as though at that time the southern basin had been free of water and exposed. When the sea level was low enough to expose the entire southern basin, this flat area underlain by salty mud must still have been a difficult one to cross. Perhaps the possible raised roadway near station C found by the soundings was constructed long ago in order to avoid a long bypass around the mud. Alternately, the feature may be a long low wall.

At diving stations A, B, D, E, and F Mr. Baney found crusts of gypsum crystals covering the muds and stones of the sea floor down to depths of at least 13 meters. Most of the submerged trees also are coated with this material, some places evenly and some places in nodular form (Fig. 5). The

A. Branch broken off submerged tree 5 meters deep at diving station B, off Khirbet Qumran. Note remnants of gypsum encrustation.

B. Uppermost twig of erect tree 1.5 meters high, from depth of 6 meters at diving station B.

C. Internal structure of gypsum crust from sea floor 6 meters deep at diving station F near the north tip of El Lisan Peninsula.

D. Internal lamination of gypsum crust of branch shown in photograph A.

crusts are layered, with each layer of gypsum a few millimeters thick and interbedded with thin layers of calcite and aragonite. All three materials are now being deposited from the waters of the Dead Sea owing to the great rate of evaporation from the sea and resulting supersaturation of some of the materials which are dissolved in the water. The layering testifies to variations in rate and nature of deposition. Probably a more complete understanding of the origin of the deposits can lead to the use of the layers as a kind of natural weather record for as many years as the layers represent.

Cores of bottom sediments (Fig. 6) were collected at three stations: A, B, and H of Figure 4. They were obtained by pounding lengths of 10 cm diameter pipe into the bottom, thereby forcing the sediment into the bottom end of the pipes. After the pipes were removed and brought back to shore, the cores were extruded into 50-cm lengths of cardboard tubing, which were wrapped and sealed for shipment to the sediment laboratory.

At station A the core was from a water depth of 1 meter atop the roadway to Rujm el-Bahr. The entire length of 135 cm consists of gray clay broken into fragments by drying joints. Salt crystals are

Figure 6. Photographs of sections of the three cores which were collected at stations A, B, and H at the Dead Sea. Each of the sections was preserved in a 50-cm cardboard tube. Numbers indicate the depth of each section below the sediment surface.

Table I
Laboratory Analyses of Sediment

Station	Depth (cm)	Median Diameter (microns)	Sorting Coefficient	Percentage of Dry Weight					
				Gravel	Sand	Silt	Clay	Calcium Carbonate	Organic Nitrogen
A	23- 27	1.3	—	0	1	29	70	30.3	0.024
	73- 77	1.7	—	0	1	35	64	32.2	0.023
	115-117	2.1	—	0	8	30	62	31.0	0.024
off A (52 m)	0- 4	4.4	3.6	0	3	49	48	28.2	0.114
B	23- 27	67.	4.6	0	52	30	18	40.3	0.018
	73- 77	19.	4.4	0	25	47	28	40.8	0.025
	125-127	6900.	2.4	77	23	0	0	—	—
	173-177	4.4	2.9	0	2	52	46	43.4	0.072
H	8- 12	6.4	2.7	0	3	58	39	42.5	0.071
	28- 32	11.	3.1	0	11	58	31	28.0	0.071
	45- 49	8300.	—	69	31	0	0	—	—

well developed within the joint planes. In the bottommost section, 100-135 cm, the clay contains some rounded pebbles to 3 cm diameter. The core at station B, off the Qumran Caves, was from a 5-meter water depth. At the top, 0 to 100 cm, the core is banded gray-white-red silt showing considerable disturbance during collection. Between 100 and 150 cm is gravel which grades from 6-cm diameter at the top to very coarse sand at the bottom. All the pebbles are subangular limestone and hard shale. The bottom of the core, 150-200 cm, consists of buff clayey silt with many 2-mm gypsum crystals. At station H a core was taken from a water depth of 4 meters. Between 0 and 20 cm it consists of buff clayey silt having traces of bedding. At 20-22 cm is a layer of rounded limestone gravel to 4 cm diameter. From 22 to 39 cm the core consists of dark gray silt having many gypsum and salt crystals. The bottom part, 39-60 cm, is of subangular gravel to 8 cm diameter embedded in a matrix of gray silty coarse sand. Lastly, a grab sample was collected from the bottom just south of station A (Fig. 4). This dive, 52 meters, is doubtlessly the deepest one yet made in the Dead Sea and it was by Mr. Baney using self-contained underwater breathing apparatus. The sediment as received is black silty clay.

Laboratory analyses (Table I) verify the visual descriptions of grain size. The finest material is from station A atop the roadway leading to Rujm el-Bahr, a flat area near the mouth of the Jordan River. Sediment obtained during the deep dive near station A is slightly coarser. The sand fraction at station A consists mostly of detrital quartz, chert, and other mineral grains brought to the sea from distant sources by the Jordan River. Much coarser sediment at mid-depths in cores from stations B and H consists of limestone pebbles and granules brought to the sea from nearby outcrops by stream or wave erosion and concentrated by winnowing at shorelines of former low sea levels. It is associated with chert derived from the same outcrops. At station B these sediments also contain many fossil foraminifera, some of which have been replaced by chert. They consist of species characteristic of the Late Cretaceous Period, about 75 million years ago. Their abundant presence in modern sediments of the Dead Sea is ample testimony of the ease with which microfossils can be reworked from exposed strata.

The content of calcium carbonate averages 35 per cent of total dry sediment (Table 1). Some of it is in the form of the limestone debris, particularly in the coarse-grained samples, but elsewhere most of it is in fine silt and clay sizes, especially at station A, and this material was chemically precipitated from surface water. During the summers of 1943 and 1959 the sea was observed to become milky with fine-grained calcium carbonate precipitated because of supersaturation resulting from high water temperatures. Precipitation probably also occurred during other summers but to a lesser degree and it was not observed or at least not recorded.

Another kind of chemical precipitate occurs in the sand fractions of the sediments of each station and is dominant at station H. This is gypsum in the form of rosettes, lens shaped opaque white, and 0.5 to 2 mm in diameter. Their abundance, particularly at station H, is an indication of the precipitation of calcium sulfate from bottom water because of supersaturation resulting from evaporation.

In each sample, and particularly in the one for the deep dive off station A, there are wood fibers and a few seed cases. These materials are not from growth within the sea, but instead they are washed in by streams, particularly by the Jordan River. The fibers account for the presence of organic nitrogen (Table I), which ranges from 0.018 to 0.114 per cent of total dry sediment. The average, 0.049 per cent, corresponds to about 0.8 per cent total organic matter. Although this concentration is much lower than in most marine sediments, it is sufficient to serve as food for indigenous sulfate-reducing bacteria whose activities deplete both sulfate and dissolved oxygen and release hydrogen sulfide to the deeper waters of the sea.

These topographic and sedimentary data provide only the barest outline of what can be learned by a more complete study. Both kinds of data can be useful to archaeologists and historians as well as to geologists who see the Dead Sea as a model for studying the processes of salt and gypsum deposition. To the archaeologists, sounding and diving observations during a later expedition should reveal the nature of the linear feature in the southern basin and its relationship to known village sites and to possible submerged ones. To the geologists new cores and soundings will reveal some of the history of the Dead Sea as recorded by deposits formed at high water levels and by erosions at low levels.

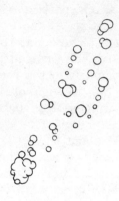